Granny's

Incredible Edibles Cookbook

This cookbook is dedicated to the memory of my grandmother, Elizabeth. "Granny" always loved to keep our stomachs full and our hearts happy, with the wonderful food and treats from her "magical" kitchen. We will be forever grateful...

...and also dedicated to the other great gourmet cook in the family, my mother, Liga, who patiently helped with the editing of this cookbook, so that you could also enjoy granny's incredible cooking...

Peter

Peter Roberts

Granny's

Incredible Edibles Cookbook

Edited by Peter Roberts

 Goldtree Press

Library of Congress Catalog Card Number: 94-76784
ISBN 0-9641565-5-5

Published By:

Goldtree Press
1174 South Diamond Bar Boulevard, Suite 631
Diamond Bar, California 91765

9 8 7 6 5 4 3 2 1
Digit on the right is the number of this printing.

Printed in the United States of America

MENU

Introduction

Thank you for letting me share with you this special collection of favorite recipes from my grandmother. *Granny's Incredible Edibles Cookbook* offers you over 200 mouth-watering recipes. You will discover delicious American, international, old-fashioned, country-style and unusual recipes. You will find these recipes extraordinarily palate-pleasing, yet quick and easy-to-prepare using simple instructions and common ingredients.

You will enjoy these incredible recipes for breakfast, lunch, dinner, snacks, parties, picnics, holidays, romantic dinners or anytime. You will love the tasty appetizers, salads and dressings, main dishes, vegetables, side dishes, breads, pies, cakes, cookies, candies and desserts. Whether you are a first-time or an experienced cook, you will discover new, exciting and unique recipes that surely will impress your family and friends, and get you rave reviews.

Granny had "retired" from her "magical" kitchen in her later years, but occasionally she was still spotted in the kitchen helping make her famous bacon rolls, or passing along cooking secrets to the "youngsters." Although granny has left us, she lives on in our hearts and will never be forgotten.

May you find lots of joy and happiness from these special recipes as our family has for so many years. I would love to hear how you and your family enjoy them...

Peter Roberts

Appetizers

Cheese Puffs

    2   cups Swiss cheese, grated
3/4 cup flour
1/2 cup butter, melted
      Salt and pepper to taste
      Whipped cream

    Mix all ingredients together well, except whipped cream. Form into balls. Press flat on a cookie sheet. Glaze with whipped cream. Bake at 450° for 7 minutes.

Nutty Cheese Balls

    1   cup sharp Cheddar cheese, shredded
1/4 cup butter
1/2 cup flour
1/4 teaspoon salt
    1   cup filberts, ground
    1   teaspoon paprika

    Mix together well the cheese, butter, flour, salt, half of the filberts and paprika. Form teaspoonfuls of the dough into little balls. Roll balls in the remaining filberts and place on cookie sheet. Chill. Bake at 350° for 10 minutes, or until lightly browned.

Herbed Cheese Balls

        1   pound sharp Cheddar cheese, shredded
      1/2   cup soft butter
      1/2   cup sherry
        3   tablespoons parsley, minced
        3   tablespoons chives, minced
        2   tablespoons tarragon, minced
            Salt and pepper to taste
      1/2   cup walnuts, chopped

Mix together well the cheese, butter, sherry, parsley, chives and tarragon. Add salt and pepper. Form into balls and roll in the chopped nuts. Chill in refrigerator. Put on toothpicks and serve.

Cheese Potato Chips

The only thing easier than making these is to boil water...

        Potato chips of your choice
        Parmesan cheese, grated

Spread potato chips on a baking pan. Sprinkle chips generously with cheese. Bake at 400° for 5 minutes.

Onion Cheese Canapés

       12   bread rounds
       12   thin slices of white onion
      1/4   cup mayonnaise
      1/4   teaspoon curry powder
        2   tablespoons Parmesan cheese, grated

Place bread rounds on a cookie sheet. Put a very thin onion slice on each. Mix together mayonnaise and curry powder; spread on top. Sprinkle with cheese. Brown under broiler and serve.

Cottage Cheese Canapés

Rye bread or other whole-grain bread, sliced and
cut into shapes

Butter
- 1/2 cup cottage cheese
- 1 teaspoon caraway seeds
- 1 teaspoon chives, chopped

Lemon juice to taste
Salt to taste
Paprika
Parsley, chopped
Clear aspic

Fry the bread in butter. Put cheese through a sieve and
combine with the next 5 ingredients. Spread the mixture over the
fried bread pieces. Garnish with parsley. Glaze with clear aspic.
Chill and serve.

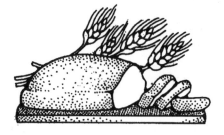

Peanut Butter Cheese Sandwiches

Bread of your choice, sliced
Mayonnaise
Peanut butter
Cheddar cheese, sliced

Spread mayonnaise on bread. Top with peanut butter. Place a
thin slice of cheese on top. Place sandwiches in a 400° oven until
the cheese is bubbly.

Latvian Cheese

2	large cartons of cottage cheese
10	eggs
4	cups milk
1	cup water
2	cups buttermilk
1	teaspoon caraway seeds
1	cube butter
	Salt to taste

Put cottage cheese and eggs in a food processor and mix until smooth. Pour milk, water and buttermilk into a pot and heat until separated. Add cottage cheese mixture and caraway seeds. Heat until well separated.

Pour mixture into a colander lined with cheese cloth; allow to drain. Put mixture back into the pot, and mix with butter and salt. Drain once more using cheese cloth in colander. Remove cheese from colander, leaving the cheese in the cheese cloth. Wrap cheese cloth around the cheese.

Press out liquid from cheese. Put cheese on a board, and place a weight such as a 5-pound bag of flour on top. Leave weight on for 2 hours. Remove cheese from cheese cloth. Wrap cheese in plastic wrap and refrigerate.

Grilled Curry Sandwiches

1 1/2	cups Cheddar cheese, shredded
1	cup olives, chopped
1/2	cup green onions, chopped
1/2	teaspoon curry powder
1/2	teaspoon salt
1/2	cup mayonnaise
	English muffins, split

Mix together all ingredients and spread on toasted split English muffins. Broil until bubbly. Cut into quarter or half pieces.

Basil Crisps

1	small loaf French bread, sliced 1/4 inch thick
1/2	cup basil leaves, chopped
1/2	cup Parmesan cheese, grated
1	clove garlic, minced
6	tablespoons mayonnaise

Toast the sliced bread. Mix together basil leaves, cheese, garlic and mayonnaise. Spread mixture on toasted bread. Broil until bubbly.

Bacon Crisps

1   pound bacon, sliced
1   egg, slightly beaten
1   cup cereal crumbs

Cut each bacon slice into three pieces. Dip bacon pieces in the beaten egg, then in the crumbs. Fry bacon slices in butter until golden brown. They may be refrigerated and later reheated in a hot oven for 5 to 10 minutes, until crispy. Drain on paper towels before serving.

Sourdough Wafers

3   sourdough French rolls
1   cube butter
2   medium-sized garlic cloves, minced
    Dash of cayenne pepper

Slice French rolls thinly. Mix butter, garlic and cayenne pepper. Spread mixture on both sides of the slices. Place wafers on cookie sheet in oven at 300° for 45 minutes, or until slices are crisp. Store in a covered container in refrigerator.

Glazed Ham Cubes

This is a quick one to fix if you are running a bit behind schedule...

1   large 1/2-inch thick slice of cooked ham
1/3   cup chunky peanut butter

Spread peanut butter on the ham slice. Place ham under broiler for 2 to 3 minutes, or until peanut butter forms a brown crust. Cut ham slice into 1-inch squares. Serve on toothpicks while still hot from the broiler.

Bacon Rolls

Granny's rolls win first prize in the appetizer category hands down!

Filling:

- 1 pound bacon, cut into very small cubes
- 1 onion, cut into very small cubes
- 1 pound ham, cut into very small cubes
-    Salt and pepper to taste

Fry bacon in frying pan until the fat separates; drain. Turn into a large bowl. Sauté onion until transparent; add to bacon. Add other ingredients and mix well; set aside.

Basic Yeast Dough:

- 2 tablespoons dry yeast
- 1/2 cup warm water
- 1 teaspoon sugar
- 2 1/2 cups whole milk
- 2 tablespoons sugar
- 1 teaspoon salt
- 1/2 cup butter
-    Rind of 1 lemon
- 5-6 cups all-purpose flour
- 2 tablespoons sour cream
- 2 egg yolks

Add yeast to mixture of 1/2 cup warm water and 1 teaspoon sugar; let stand for 10 minutes.

In a saucepan, scald the milk. Add 2 tablespoons sugar; add salt, butter and lemon rind. Cool mixture until lukewarm. Then, add 3 1/2 cups flour, sour cream, egg yolks and yeast mixture. Beat with a wooden spoon until smooth and shiny. Cover bowl and let rise for 1 hour.

Turn out on a floured board. Add remaining 2 cups flour gradually. Knead until dough is elastic and hands come out clean. Place dough back into bowl. Cover and let rise 45 minutes longer.

Bacon Roll Preparation:

1 egg, beaten

On a floured board, roll out dough about 1/4 inch thick. Starting in one corner, place 1 teaspoon of bacon filling on the dough. Fold over. Cut into a "half-moon" shape using the edge of a drinking glass or round cookie cutter. Press the seam tightly with fingers and tuck seam under. Place rolls on a greased cookie sheet. Brush with beaten egg. Let rise 30 minutes.

Bake at 400° for 10 minutes or until golden brown. Rolls may be frozen and reheated later. Serve rolls warm.

World's Best Salsa and Chips

Basic Salsa: *(Basic Salsa must be canned after making)*

- 5 **pounds tomatoes**
- 3 **pounds chili peppers**
- 2 **pounds onions**
- 1 **tablespoon salt**
- 1 **cup vinegar or lemon juice**

Seed tomatoes and chop into small dice; tomatoes may be peeled if desired. Chop chilies; seeds may be removed if desired.

Peel and chop onions. Mix together well the tomatoes, chilies, onions and salt. Place the mixture into a large colander and drain for 1 hour.

Bring to boil in a large kettle, adding vinegar or lemon juice. Pack basic salsa in hot, sterilized jars and seal immediately. Test seals after 24 hours. Any basic salsa not properly sealed should be refrigerated and eaten within 10 days. Basic salsa can be used by itself in many other dishes.

World's Best Salsa and Chips:

- 5 **tomatoes, chopped**
- 3 **onions, chopped**
- 1 **tablespoon salt**
  Basic salsa (as prepared above)
- 1 **bunch cilantro, chopped**
- 1 **Lemon**
  Tortilla chips or crackers

Seed tomatoes and chop into small dice; tomatoes may be peeled if desired. Peel and chop onions. Mix together well the tomatoes, onions and salt. Place mixture into a large colander and drain for 1 hour.

Pour drained mixture into a bowl. Add basic salsa to taste, starting with 3/4 cup and adding more as desired. Add chopped cilantro and several squeezes of lemon juice.

Serve salsa with tortilla chips or crackers of your choice.

Nachos

Nachos are <u>always</u> a sure-fire favorite for parties...

  1   **12-ounce can Jalapeño bean dip**
  2   **packages frozen avocado dip**
  1   **cup sour cream**
1/3   **cup mayonnaise**
  2   **tablespoons dry taco seasoning**
  1   **4-ounce can black olives, chopped**
  1   **tomato, chopped and seeded**
      Green onions, chopped
  1   **pound Cheddar cheese, grated**
  1   **pound bag tortilla chips**

Spread bean dip on 9-inch platter. Thaw avocado dip and spread over bean dip. Combine sour cream, mayonnaise and taco seasoning. Spread sour cream mixture over avocado dip. Layer the remaining ingredients over the sour cream mixture in this order: olives, tomato, onions and cheese.

Serve at room temperature with tortilla chips. May be refrigerated for several hours after making.

German Meatballs

1	cup raw potato, grated
1	pound lean ground beef
	Grind of black pepper
1	tablespoon parsley, chopped
1	teaspoon seasoned salt
1	teaspoon onion, minced
1	egg, slightly beaten
3	teaspoons cornstarch
2 1/2	cups beef bouillon
1/2	teaspoon caraway seeds
1	tablespoon cold water

Mix the first 7 ingredients. Form into walnut-sized balls and roll in 2 teaspoons cornstarch.

Put bouillon in deep pot with a tight cover. Bring to a boil and drop in meatballs one at a time. Cover and simmer for 30 minutes. Remove meatballs with slotted spoon and keep hot.

Add the caraway seeds and a little freshly ground black pepper to stock in which meatballs were cooked. Simmer while uncovered for 10 minutes. Mix remaining teaspoon of cornstarch with the cold water and stir into stock. Cook while stirring until sauce is thick. Combine sauce with meatballs and serve.

Chili Meatballs

Meatballs:

- 12   soda crackers
- 1   teaspoon salt
- 1   teaspoon chili powder
- 2   tablespoons milk
- 1   egg
- 3   tablespoons onion, chopped
- 1   tablespoon butter
- 1   pound ground beef

Crush crackers and combine with salt, chili powder, milk and egg; set mixture aside.

Sauté onion in butter. Add onions and beef to cracker mixture; mix together well. Shape into walnut-sized balls. Place closely together in a single layer on a baking pan. Bake at 400° for 20 to 25 minutes until brown, turning once.

Sauce:

- 1/4   cup onions, chopped
- 1   tablespoon butter
- 1 1/2   tablespoons flour
- 2 1/2   cups beef broth
- 3/4   cup canned tomato sauce
- 1/4   teaspoon salt
- 1/4   teaspoon pepper
- 1   teaspoon chili powder

Sauté onions in butter; add flour. Stir in beef broth, tomato sauce, salt, pepper and chili powder. Simmer 15 to 20 minutes until thick. Add meatballs and simmer 10 to 15 minutes longer.

Chicken Wings

If you have ever been driving in your car and wondered why 15 chickens were hitchhiking by the side of the road, this recipe may solve the mystery...

30	chicken wings
8	tablespoons butter, melted
1 1/2	cups bread crumbs
1/2	cup Parmesan cheese, grated
1	teaspoon salt
1	teaspoon garlic powder

Remove wing tips and cut wings into two pieces. Dip chicken into melted butter. Combine bread crumbs, cheese, salt and garlic powder in a plastic bag. Shake wings in crumb mixture. Place chicken on a greased 15x10-inch baking sheet. Bake in a preheated 400° oven for 30 minutes. Serve while hot.

Deviled Eggs

10	hard-boiled eggs
	Salt and pepper to taste
3	tablespoons soft butter
1	tablespoon dry mustard
1/2	cup mayonnaise
	Parsley or dill

Cut hard-boiled eggs in half lengthwise and remove yolks. Mash the yolks. Season with salt, pepper, butter, mustard powder and mayonnaise. Stuff egg whites with mixture. Garnish with parsley or dill. Chill and serve.

Tuna-Stuffed Eggs

       12   hard-boiled eggs
        1   8-ounce can solid white tuna
      1/2   cup mayonnaise
      1/4   teaspoon salt
      1/8   teaspoon black pepper
        2   tablespoons Madeira
      1/8   teaspoon thyme
      1/3   cup pecans, chopped
        1   tablespoon parsley, chopped
            Capers
            Pimento

Cut hard-boiled eggs in half lengthwise and remove yolks. Mash the yolks. Add remaining ingredients to yolks, except capers and pimento; mix well. Stuff egg whites with mixture. Garnish with capers and pimento. Chill and serve.

Stuffed Cucumber

        1   straight cucumber
      1/2   cup tuna fish
        1   tablespoon mayonnaise
        1   teaspoon onion, grated
      1/2   teaspoon lemon juice
      1/8   teaspoon white pepper

Peel the cucumber and scoop out the center with a corer. Mash the tuna fine. Mix tuna with mayonnaise, onion, lemon juice and pepper. Stuff the cucumber with this mixture and chill. Cut into 1/2 inch thick slices.

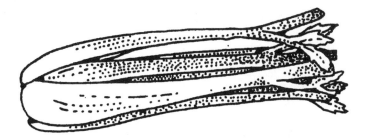

Stuffed Celery

2   3-ounce packages cream cheese
1/2 cup creamy or chunky peanut butter
1/4 cup sesame seeds, toasted
2   teaspoons milk
2   teaspoons soy sauce
1/4 teaspoon ground ginger
     Celery stalks

In a small bowl, stir together cream cheese and peanut butter until blended. Mix in sesame seeds, milk, soy sauce and ginger. Stuff celery stalks and cut into pieces.

Curried Olives

1   small loaf French bread, sliced and toasted one side
1   4-ounce can ripe olives, chopped
1/4 cup green onion, diced
3/4 cup Cheddar cheese, grated
4   tablespoons mayonnaise
     Pinch of salt
     Curry powder to taste
     Parsley, minced

Mix together the olives, onion, cheese, mayonnaise, salt and curry powder. Spread mixture on the untoasted side of French bread slices. Broil until bubbly. Sprinkle minced parsley on top.

Stuffed Mushrooms

1 pound medium-sized mushrooms
2 tablespoons butter
1 tablespoon parsley, finely chopped
1 teaspoon shallots, finely chopped
1 garlic clove, finely chopped
Dash of salt
Dash of freshly ground pepper

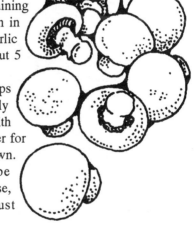

Wash mushrooms and remove stems. Save 12 of best caps for stuffing. Finely chop the remaining mushrooms and stems. Brown in butter with parsley, shallots, garlic clove, salt and pepper for about 5 minutes. Set the mixture aside.

Brown the mushroom caps on both sides for approximately 2 minutes. Stuff mushrooms with the mixture. Place under broiler for about 5 minutes, or until brown. The mushrooms may also be refrigerated until ready for use, and put under the broiler just before serving.

Crispy Avocado Cubes

1 large avocado, cubed
Lemon juice
4 tablespoons butter
1/2 teaspoon curry powder
1 cup cornflakes, crushed

Sprinkle lemon juice over avocado cubes. Melt butter, and blend in curry powder. Dip avocado cubes in the butter mixture, then into the crushed cornflakes. Serve on toothpicks.

Crab Puffs

8	ounces cream cheese, room temperature
4	tablespoons mayonnaise
1/2	pound crab meat, shredded
1	medium-size onion, finely minced
1	clove garlic, finely minced
	Salt and white pepper to taste

With the cream cheese at room temperature, blend it together with the mayonnaise. Add the crab meat, onion and garlic. Salt and pepper to taste. Buy small puffs at your favorite bakery and stuff them with the mixture.

Caviar Pie

2 cups sour cream
Juice of 1 lemon
2 tablespoons chives, chopped
8 ounces caviar
1 7-inch pie shell, baked

Put sour cream into a cloth and hang up to drain overnight. Just before serving, add lemon juice to sour cream. Spread mixture into pie shell. Sprinkle with chives. Spread caviar carefully over the top. Cut into small slices and serve.

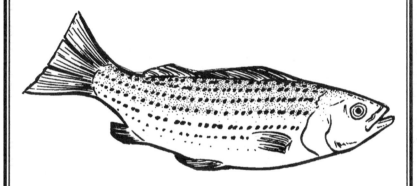

Salmon Balls

1 16-ounce can salmon, flaked
8 ounces cream cheese, softened
1 tablespoon lemon juice
2 teaspoons parsley, chopped
2 teaspoons onion, chopped
1 teaspoon horseradish
1/2 cup pecans, chopped

Combine all ingredients in a blender. Form into balls. Chill in refrigerator. Serve with crackers.

Salmon Mousse

1	envelope gelatin
1/4	cup cold water
1	bouillon cube
1/2	cup boiling water
1/2	cup mayonnaise
1/2	cup sour cream
1	tablespoon lemon juice
1	teaspoon Worcestershire sauce
1	tablespoon chives, chopped
1/2	teaspoon salt
	Dash of pepper
2	cups salmon

Mix together all of the ingredients, except salmon. Chill mixture in refrigerator until thick. Beat salmon and add to mixture. Serve in individual bowls.

Dilled Shrimp

These shrimp are so good, they just seem to "swim" off the plate and disappear as soon as you put them out...

1 1/2	cups mayonnaise
1/3	cup lemon juice
1/4	cup sugar
1/2	cup sour cream
1	large red onion, thinly sliced
2	tablespoons dry dill
1/4	teaspoon salt
2	pounds medium shrimp, cooked

In a large bowl, mix together mayonnaise, lemon juice, sugar, sour cream, onion, dill and salt. Stir shrimp into mixture. Cover and refrigerate overnight. The next day, stir a few times and serve with toothpicks.

Shrimp Mousse

1 1/2	teaspoons plain gelatin
1/2	cup cold water
3/4	cup white wine
1	8-ounce can shrimp
1	cup mayonnaise
1	tablespoon onion, chopped
1	teaspoon lemon juice
1/2	teaspoon dry mustard
	Dash cayenne pepper
	Salt to taste

Soften gelatin in water. Heat white wine and stir in the gelatin until dissolved; set aside mixture.

Place all the remaining ingredients in a blender and mix until smooth. Stir in wine mixture. Pour into a mold. Chill in refrigerator until firm. Remove from mold onto a cold platter. Garnish with lettuce and cherry tomatoes as desired.

Salads
&
Dressings

Tossed Green Salad

To prevent a big mess in your kitchen, please remember that a "tossed salad" is used only as a figure of speech...

- 1 **large ripe avocado**
- 1 **tablespoon vinegar**
- 1 **tablespoon lemon juice**
- 1/2 **teaspoon salt**
- 3/4 **teaspoon sugar**
- 1 **tablespoon onion, grated**
- 1 **clove garlic, minced**
- 1 **cup sour cream**
- 3 **tablespoons Parmesan cheese, grated**

Mash the avocado with a fork. Mix avocado together with all other ingredients. Keep in refrigerator for at least several hours. When ready to serve, mix together with the following:

- 1 **head romaine lettuce**
- 1 **head iceberg lettuce**
- 5 **small green onions, sliced**
- 1 1/2 **cups garlic-flavored croutons**
- 3 **hard-boiled eggs, coarsely chopped**
     Fresh ground pepper

Skillet Salad

5 slices bacon
1/4 cup white vinegar
2 tablespoons water
2 tablespoons sugar
1/2 teaspoon salt
Lettuce
Dash of pepper
1 hard-boiled egg, finely chopped
Green onions, minced
Avocado, diced

Fry the bacon until crisp. Remove from pan and drain on paper towels.

Combine vinegar, water, sugar and salt with bacon fat in pan. Heat to boiling; cool slightly. Pour over lettuce. Add crumbled bacon, pepper, egg, onions and avocado. Toss salad and serve.

Hot Chicken Salad

2 cups cooked chicken breasts, diced
1 1/2 cups celery, thinly sliced
1/2 cup slivered almonds, toasted
1 tablespoon onion, grated
1 cup mayonnaise
2 tablespoons lemon juice

Topping:

1 cup Cheddar cheese, grated
1 cup potato chips, finely crushed

Combine the chicken, celery, almonds, onion, mayonnaise and lemon juice in a saucepan. Warm gently over low heat; but do not overheat. Put into a greased casserole. Sprinkle with the cheese and potato chips. Place in a 450° oven for 10 minutes, or until lightly browned.

Caesar Salad

1	head romaine lettuce
1/2	teaspoon salt
1/2	teaspoon pepper, freshly ground
1/2	teaspoon dry mustard
1/4	cup olive oil
1	teaspoon lemon juice
2	tablespoons red wine vinegar
1	cup croutons
3	strips bacon, crisp and broken into small pieces
1/4	cup Parmesan cheese
1	egg

Tear up head of lettuce in a bowl. Add salt and pepper; toss. Sprinkle with dry mustard; toss. Pour in olive oil, lemon juice and vinegar; toss. Add the croutons, bacon pieces and cheese; toss again. Lastly, add egg and toss salad until egg is mixed in well. Serve salad immediately.

Shrimp Salad

1	can tomato soup
1	large package cream cheese
2	envelopes plain gelatin, dissolved in 1/2 cup water
1	cup mayonnaise
1	medium green pepper, chopped
1	cup celery, chopped
1	medium onion, chopped fine
2	cans shrimp
2	teaspoons lemon juice
	Salt and pepper to taste

Heat tomato soup. Stir in cream cheese. Add dissolved gelatin to mixture. After cooled, add mayonnaise, green pepper, celery, onions and shrimp. Add lemon juice and seasonings to taste. Place into a mold. Let stand overnight in refrigerator.

Crab Louie

    3/4   **pound crab meat**
      1   **teaspoon chives, chopped**
      2   **hard-boiled eggs, diced**

Dressing:

    1/2   **cup French dressing**
    1/2   **cup chili sauce**
      1   **teaspoon Worcestershire sauce**
      2   **tablespoons mayonnaise**
    1/2   **teaspoon salt**
          Dash of pepper

Mix all ingredients of dressing together well.

Arrange crab in a bowl or on separate plates. Sprinkle chives and eggs over top. Pour dressing over salad and serve.

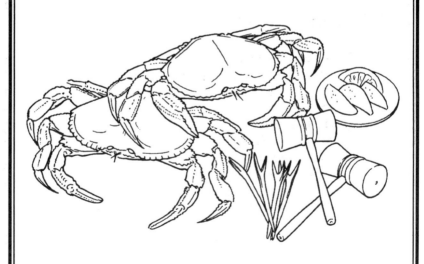

Carrot Salad

This is great for your eyes, because rabbits never wear glasses...

- **1 cup raw carrots, grated**
- **1 cup raw cabbage, chopped**
- **1 tablespoon lemon juice**
- **1/2 teaspoon salt**
- **Mayonnaise**
- **Lettuce leaves**

Mix together well the carrots, cabbage, lemon juice, salt and mayonnaise; adding enough mayonnaise to moisten all. Serve on lettuce leaves.

Cole Slaw

- **1 white head cabbage, shredded**
- **2 tablespoons sugar**
- **1 cup sour cream**
- **1 tablespoon mayonnaise**
- **1 1/2 tablespoons tarragon vinegar**
- **Salt and pepper to taste**

Shred cabbage very finely. Cool for an hour or more in ice water until crisp; drain and dry with paper towels. Mix the remaining ingredients together and toss with cabbage. Serve cold.

Cabbage Salad

4 cups cabbage, sliced
4 tablespoons green onions, diced
2 tablespoons sesame seeds
1/4 cup almond, slivered
Noodles from Top Ramen noodle soup

Dressing:

Seasoning from Top Ramen noodle soup
1/4 cup vinegar
1/2 cup salad oil
1/4 cup sugar

Mix all ingredients of dressing together.

Combine all salad ingredients together, except noodles. Crush uncooked noodles from noodle soup. When ready to serve, toss dressing and noodles into salad mixture.

Guacamole Salad

2 ripe avocados
2 tablespoons lemon juice
1 1/2 teaspoons salt
1 teaspoon black pepper
1 clove garlic, grated
1/4 cup green onions, chopped
1/4 cup green pepper, chopped
Salad greens
Tomato, cubed
Green olives, sliced
French dressing

Peel avocados and mash pulp thoroughly. Add lemon juice, salt, pepper and clove garlic. Beat in the chopped onions and green peppers. Spread avocado mixture over the salad greens. Top with tomato cubes and green olive slices. Serve with French dressing.

Potato Salad

This one is perfect for picnics and barbecues...

5   **cups boiled potatoes, diced**
1   **cup hard-boiled eggs, diced**
1   **cup dill pickles, diced**
1/2 **cup celery, diced**
1/2 **tablespoon parsley, chopped**
1   **tablespoon onions, chopped**

Dressing:

1/2 **cup salad dressing**
1/2 **cup sour cream**
1   **teaspoon mustard powder**
    Salt and pepper to taste

Mix all ingredients of dressing together.

Combine all salad ingredients together. Pour dressing over all, mixing thoroughly with a wooden spoon and fork. Keep in a cool place for several hours before serving.

Apple and Ham Salad

3   **cups tart apples, cubed**
2   **cups cooked ham, cubed**
1/2 **cup celery, diced**
1/4 **cup mayonnaise**
2   **tablespoons light cream**
1   **tablespoon lemon juice**

Combine apples, ham and celery; set aside.

Blend together the remaining ingredients. Mix this dressing mixture lightly with the apple-ham mixture.

Rice and Turkey Salad

Another great way to get rid of all those pesky turkey leftovers...

- 3 **cups rice, cooked**
- 3 **cups turkey, diced**
- 1 **cup green pepper, chopped**
- 1 **cup celery, sliced**
- 1 **can water chestnuts, sliced**

Dressing:

- 3/4 **cup mayonnaise**
- 1/4 **cup lemon juice**
- 1 **teaspoon lemon peel**
- 1 **tablespoon horseradish**
- 1 **tablespoon prepared mustard**
- 1/4 **teaspoon garlic powder**
- 1/4 **cup parsley, chopped**
- 1/2 **cup green onion, sliced**
- 2 **ounces pimiento, chopped**

Mix all salad ingredients together.

Blend together well all ingredients of dressing. Pour over salad and serve.

Macaroni and Cheese Salad

1	cup elbow macaroni
1	12-ounce can ham, cut into strips and chopped
1	cup sharp Cheddar cheese, cubed
1/2	cup celery, sliced and chopped
1/3	cup green pepper, chopped
1/4	cup green onions, sliced
2	tablespoons pimento, chopped
1/4	cup pickle relish, drained
1/2	cup mayonnaise
1	tablespoon mustard
1/4	teaspoon salt
	Salad greens

Cook and drain macaroni; allow to cool. Combine macaroni with ham, cheese, celery, green pepper, onions, pimento and relish. Blend together mayonnaise, mustard, and salt; combine with other ingredients. Toss the salad lightly. Chill in refrigerator. Serve on salad greens.

Wild Rice Fruit Salad

1/2	cup raisins
1/2	cup apricots, chopped
3/4	cup wild rice, cooked
3/4	cup red grapes, halved
3/4	cup toasted walnuts, chopped
4	green onions, sliced
1/3	cup chives, chopped
4	tablespoons parsley, chopped
2	teaspoons honey
	Juice of 1 lemon
5	tablespoons olive oil
2	teaspoons mint, chopped
	Salt and pepper to taste

Cover raisins and apricots with boiling water for 30 minutes. Drain. Add cooked wild rice, red grapes, walnuts, green onions, chives and parsley. Mix all together well. Combine honey, lemon juice, olive oil and mint. Mix with dry ingredients.

Ranch Salad Dressing

1	onion, minced
1	clove garlic, minced
5	cups mayonnaise
3	cups sour cream
1/2	teaspoon pepper
2	teaspoons seasoned salt
1/4	cup dill weed
1/4	cup parsley
	Juice of 2 lemons
1/8	teaspoon Tabasco sauce

In a large bowl, combine all ingredients. Blend with mixer until light and fluffy. Refrigerate for several hours before serving. Dressing will keep in refrigerator for about one week.

Roquefort Dressing

3/4 pound Roquefort cheese
2 cups mayonnaise
1 cup sour cream
1/2 teaspoon lemon juice
1 small onion, grated

Mash cheese in mixer. Add mayonnaise, sour cream, lemon juice and onion. Mix at low speed until combined; keep lumps in.

Thousand Island Dressing

1/4 cup chili sauce
1 cup mayonnaise
2 hard-boiled eggs, chopped
2 tablespoons celery, chopped
1 tablespoon green peppers, chopped
1 green onion, chopped
1/2 teaspoon salt
1/2 teaspoon paprika

Combine all ingredients in a bowl. Mix well until blended. Cover and refrigerate.

French Dressing

1/2 cup olive oil
2 tablespoons vinegar
2 tablespoons lemon juice
1/2 teaspoon salt
1 teaspoon sugar
1/2 teaspoon dry mustard
Dash of pepper
Dash of paprika

Combine all ingredients in a jar. Cover and shake well. Chill.

Italian Dressing

- 1 **cup olive oil**
- 1/4 **cup vinegar**
- 1 **teaspoon salt**
- 1/2 **teaspoon white pepper**
- 1 **clove garlic, minced**
- 1/4 **teaspoon cayenne pepper**
- 1/4 **teaspoon dry mustard**

Combine all ingredients in a jar. Cover and shake well. Chill.

Granny's Famous Hamburgers

Cook granny's hamburgers rare for the juiciest and greatest taste!

- 1 **pound lean ground beef**
- 1 **tablespoon mayonnaise**
- 1 **tablespoon water**
- 1 **teaspoon Worcestershire sauce**
- 1 **teaspoon salt**
- 1/4 **teaspoon pepper**

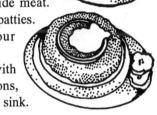

Gently mix the ground beef with mayonnaise, water, Worcestershire sauce, salt and pepper. Using a kitchen fork, divide meat. Shape and flatten loosely into 4 thick patties. Fry, grill or broil hamburgers to your desired doneness.

Put hamburger on a bun, and top with your choice of lettuce, tomatoes, onions, pickles, ketchup, mustard or the kitchen sink.

Sloppy Joes

- 1 **pound ground beef**
- 1 **cup onions, chopped**
- 1 **10-ounce can condensed tomato soup, undiluted**
- 1/4 **cup water**
- 1 **tablespoon Worcestershire sauce**
- 3/4 **teaspoon salt**
- 1/2 **teaspoon oregano**
  Dash of red pepper sauce
- 6 **hamburger buns**

In a frying pan, cook beef until brown. Add onions and sauté for about 5 minutes. Spoon off drippings. Add the next 6 ingredients. Cover, bring to boiling over medium heat. Reduce heat and simmer for 30 minutes, stirring occasionally. Spread mixture onto hamburger buns and enjoy.

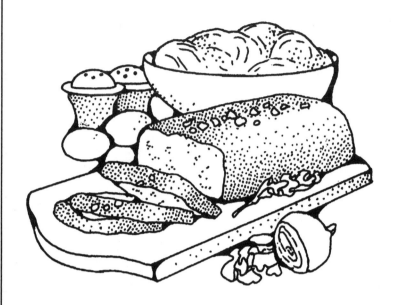

Meat Loaf

1 1/2	pounds ground beef
1	cup dry bread crumbs
1 1/4	cups milk
1	egg, beaten
1/4	cup onion, minced
1/4	teaspoon pepper
1 1/4	teaspoons salt
1/4	teaspoon dry mustard
1/4	teaspoon celery salt
1/4	teaspoon garlic salt
1	tablespoon Worcestershire sauce
2	slices of bacon
2	tablespoons catsup

Combine first 11 ingredients. Shape into a loaf on a shallow baking pan. Put 2 slices of bacon on top lengthwise. Spread catsup on top. Bake at 350° about 1 1/2 hours, or until done. Serve hot.

Chili Con Carne

2 pounds ground round steak
2 tablespoons butter
2 green peppers
2 onions, sliced
2 cans kidney beans
1 can tomato soup
2 tablespoons chili powder
Salt and pepper to taste

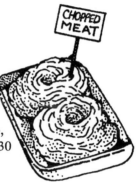

Brown meat in butter. Add green peppers and onions. Cook until onions are tender. Add kidney beans, tomato soup, chili powder, salt and pepper. Simmer 30 minutes. Serve hot with crackers or toast.

Pepper Steak

1 pound beef chuck
1/4 cup cooking oil
1 clove garlic, minced
1 tablespoon soy sauce
1 teaspoon salt
1 1/4 cups water
1 cup green pepper, cut into pieces
1/2 cup celery, chopped
1 cup onion, chopped
1 tablespoon cornstarch
2 tomatoes, cut into thin wedges

Cut beef into thin strips. Brown beef in oil. Add garlic and cook until yellow. Add soy sauce, salt and 1/4 cup water; cook 45 minutes. Add vegetables and cook 10 minutes, or until both meat and vegetables are tender. Stir in cornstarch blended with 1 cup water. Then, add tomatoes and cook for 5 minutes. Serve over fluffy rice.

Southern Barbecued Steak

- 1/4   **cup soft butter**
- 2   **tablespoons dry mustard**
- 2   **teaspoons salt**
- 1/4   **teaspoon pepper**
- 3/4   **teaspoon paprika**
- 2   **teaspoons sugar**
- 2   **pounds sirloin steak, 1-inch thick**
- 1/4   **cup olive oil**
- 2   **tablespoons Worcestershire sauce**
- 2   **tablespoons catsup**
- 3/4   **teaspoon salt**
- 3/4   **teaspoon sugar**

Prepare seasoned butter by mixing the first 6 ingredients. Spread half of seasoned butter on one side of steak. In a large frying pan, brown meat buttered side down. As this browns, spread remaining butter over top; turn and brown. Place steaks in a broiler pan.

Prepare sauce by mixing together the remaining ingredients and pan drippings. Brush steak with sauce. Broil 6 inches from heat about 5 to 7 minutes on each side, brushing often with sauce.

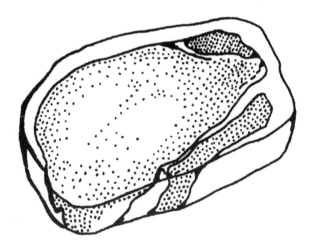

Filet Mignon

4 filet mignon steaks, 2-inches thick
Butter, softened
Onion and garlic salt
Dash of Accent

Allow steaks to reach room temperature. Preheat broiler 10 minutes. Spread both sides of steaks with softened butter. Sprinkle with onion and garlic salt, and a dash of Accent.

Grease rack and broil the steaks for 20 to 25 minutes for medium done; turning steaks over after about 15 minutes when first side is done. Brush steaks with extra butter and serve.

Veal Casserole

4	**pounds veal, cubed**
4	**tablespoons butter**
2	**onions, chopped**
2	**cloves garlic**
2	**cups chicken stock**
2	**tablespoons tomato paste**
1 1/2	**tablespoons paprika**
1	**teaspoon oregano**
2	**teaspoons salt**
1	**bay leaf**
2	**cups sour cream**
1/2	**cup white wine**
1	**pound mushrooms**

Brown the veal in butter. Place in a casserole. Sauté onions and garlic; add chicken stock, tomato paste, paprika, oregano, salt and bay leaf. Pour mixture over the veal. Cook covered at 325° for 1 1/2 hours.

Mix the sour cream with white wine; add to veal. Sauté mushrooms in butter; add to veal.

Lasagne

1/2	pound lasagne noodles
1	pound ground beef
1/2	cup onion, chopped
3	cloves garlic, minced
1	tablespoon olive oil
3	pounds tomatoes; peeled, seeded and chopped
1 1/2	teaspoons seasoned salt
1/4	teaspoon freshly ground pepper
3	tablespoons parsley, chopped
1/2	teaspoon oregano
1	teaspoon basil

Cook noodles in salted, boiling water until firm. Drain and place noodles in cold water until ready to use.

Sauté ground beef, onion and garlic in olive oil until meat is not pink. Add tomatoes, salt, pepper, parsley, oregano and basil. Cook at a fast simmer for 30 to 35 minutes until sauce is thick. Spoon off fat. Preheat oven to 400°.

White Sauce:

1/2	cup butter
4	tablespoons flour
1	cup milk
1	cup chicken broth
1/8	teaspoon salt

Melt butter. Add flour and cook one minute while stirring. Slowly add milk and chicken broth; bring to a boil while stirring. Add salt.

Ricotta Filling:

1	egg
1/4	cup Parmesan cheese, grated
1/2	pound ricotta cheese
1/8	teaspoon nutmeg
1/2	teaspoon salt

Beat egg in a bowl. Add cheeses, nutmeg and salt while stirring well.

Cheese:

1 1/2 cups Parmesan cheese, grated
4 ounces teleme cheese
4 ounces mozzarella cheese, sliced
Butter

Layer in a greased 9x13-inch baking dish in this order: A little meat sauce, half of the noodles, half of the remaining meat sauce, 1/2 cup white sauce, 1/2 cup Parmesan cheese, half of the mozzarella, teleme and ricotta; the remaining noodles and meat sauce, 1/2 cup white sauce, 1/2 cup Parmesan, the remaining mozzarella, teleme, ricotta, white sauce, and Parmesan cheeses. Dot with butter. Dish may be covered and refrigerated.

From room temperature, bake uncovered at 400° for at least 30 minutes, until bubbly. This dish freezes very well.

Beef Stew

2	pounds beef stew meat
	Flour
	Salt and pepper
2	cans beef broth
1	cup red wine
1	stalk celery, chopped
1	bay leaf
1/2	onion, chopped
2	cloves garlic, minced
1	teaspoon thyme
1	tablespoon Worcestershire sauce
1	can tomato stew
5	carrots, sliced
1	pound small white onions

Dust meat with flour, salt and pepper. Brown meat in pan. Then, place into a Dutch oven. Cover meat with beef broth, red wine, celery and bay leaf. Add chopped onions, garlic, thyme and Worcestershire sauce. Stir in stewed tomatoes.

Cover and cook in oven at 350° for 2 to 2 1/2 hours until meat is tender; 40 minutes before meat is done, add carrots and small white onions. If gravy is too thin, thicken with cornstarch.

Beef Stroganoff

3	tablespoons butter
1 1/2	pounds top sirloin, cut into strips
3	small onions
1/2	pound mushrooms, sliced
1 1/2	cups beef broth
1	teaspoon salt
1/8	teaspoon pepper
1 1/2	teaspoons Worcestershire sauce
	Sherry to taste
1	cup sour cream

Melt butter in frying pan. Sear sirloin and onions over high heat. Then, add sautéed mushrooms, broth, salt, pepper and Worcestershire sauce. Remove from heat and allow to cool. Add sherry to taste. Add sour cream and reheat; but do not boil. Serve with noodles or rice.

Stroganoff may be refrigerated or it may be frozen to serve later. Reheat. Add sour cream and reheat again; but do not boil.

Spareribs

Do meat markets only sell "spareribs" because the "regular ribs" are so darn good that your butcher is always sold out?

4	pounds spareribs
3/4	cup orange juice concentrate
1 1/2	teaspoons Worcestershire sauce
1/2	teaspoon garlic salt
1/8	teaspoon pepper

Place ribs in shallow roasting pan, meaty side down. Roast in oven at 450° for 30 minutes; drain fat. Turn ribs and roast an additional 30 minutes; drain fat. Combine orange juice, Worcestershire sauce, garlic salt and pepper; brush on ribs. Reduce heat to 350°. Cover and roast ribs for 1 hour or until tender, brushing with sauce.

Baked Ham

   1   smoked ham
   2   cups dark brown sugar
   2   cups vinegar
       Currant Jelly
       Bread crumbs

   Boil the ham in water to which the brown sugar and vinegar have been added. When tender, remove from water and allow ham to cool.

   Skin the ham. Coat with a layer of currant jelly mixed with bread crumbs. Brown ham in 350° oven. Slice and serve.

Ham and Potatoes

   6   raw potatoes, sliced
       Flour
   1   pound raw smoked ham
   3   cups milk

   Cover the bottom of a greased baking dish with sliced raw potatoes. Sprinkle with flour. Add a layer of 1-inch square pieces of ham. Repeat the above until dish is full. Pour milk into dish until it is full (3 cups or more). Bake at 350° for 1 to 1 1/2 hours, until potatoes are tender.

Baked Pork Chops

6	pork chops
1	teaspoon salt
1/8	teaspoon pepper
2	8-ounce cans tomato sauce
1/2	cup water
1/2	cup celery, finely chopped
1	tablespoon brown sugar
1	teaspoon prepared mustard
	Juice of 1/2 lemon
	Vegetable oil

Sprinkle pork chops with salt and pepper. Brown chops in hot oil in a frying pan. Place pork chops into a shallow baking dish. Combine the remaining ingredients and pour over chops. Cover and bake at 350° for 1 to 1 1/4 hours, or until tender.

Quiche

Granny's quiche is so irresistible, even _real_ men will eat it!

1 1/2	cups Swiss cheese, grated
1	3-ounce jar mushrooms, sliced and drained
12	bacon strips, fried and crumbled
1	cup whipping cream
1/2	cup milk
3	eggs, beaten
1/8	teaspoon pepper
	Dash of cayenne
	Pastry for 10-inch pie, unbaked

Line 10-inch pie pan with pastry. Sprinkle bottom with grated cheese. Sprinkle on sliced mushrooms, followed by crumbled bacon. Combine whipping cream, milk, eggs, pepper and cayenne. Pour mixture into shell. Bake at 375° for 35 minutes or until light brown and set.

Chicken Kiev

A classic, unforgettable and all-time family favorite...

- 3   **boned chicken breasts**
- 1   **cup unsalted butter, well chilled**
- 2   **tablespoons parsley, chopped**
- 2   **tablespoons green onions, chopped**
- 1   **cup flour**
- 1   **egg**
- 2   **cups bread crumbs**
-    **Salt and pepper to taste**

Split the chicken breasts. Pound the chicken between sheets of wax paper until 1/4 inch thick.

Knead butter into rolls about 2 inches long and 1/2 inch thick. Chill these thoroughly; placing them in the freezer for a few hours.

Place 1 teaspoon parsley, 1 teaspoon green onions, and a butter roll 1 to 2 inches from the lower edge of chicken breast half. Fold edge of breast over filling. Fold in each side to enclose filling; then roll up chicken over and around the filling into a bundle. Fasten it firmly with toothpicks. Try to surround the butter completely with the chicken meat so that no butter will leak out during cooking.

Setup 3 plates: one with flour, one with beaten egg in a little water, and one with fine bread crumbs seasoned to taste with salt and pepper. First, roll the chicken in the flour. Then, roll in the beaten egg, coating chicken completely. Lastly, roll the chicken in the bread crumbs until entire surface is covered. Firmly pat crumbs in place. Refrigerate chicken for at least an hour to set the bread crumbs.

Deep fry chicken in vegetable oil at 375°, 3 or 4 at a time for approximately 5 minutes; turning often and frying until golden brown. Drain chicken on paper towels.

Place chicken in pan, cover with aluminum foil and place in oven at 350° for 10 to 15 minutes, until chicken is no longer pink when cut. Make only a shallow cut, so the filling doesn't leak out.

And the toothpicks... don't forget to take out the toothpicks!

Roast Chicken

4	**pound chicken**
1/2	**lemon**
1/2	**pound butter**
	Salt
	Pepper
3	**tablespoons flour**
3/4	**cup cream**
1	**cup chicken stock**
1	**teaspoon tarragon**

Preheat oven to 425°.

Wipe the chicken using paper towels. Rub lemon inside. Cream together 4 tablespoons butter, 1 teaspoon salt and 1/2 teaspoon pepper. Place mixture into cavity.

Truss bird and sew up the cavity. Rub one side with butter. Place chicken on its side, buttered side up. Roast 20 minutes. Turn over and brush with melted butter. Roast 20 minutes. Turn on back and baste with drippings. Sprinkle with 1 teaspoon salt and 1 teaspoon pepper. Roast 20 minutes.

To make sauce, remove drippings from pan and stir in the flour, cream and chicken stock. Season with tarragon and salt.

Barbecued Chicken Legs

> 8 chicken legs
> 1/4 cup barbecue sauce
> 1 tablespoon frozen orange juice
> 1 tablespoon honey

Combine barbecue sauce, orange juice and honey. Place chicken legs in a baking pan; brush with sauce. Cook at 450° for 5 minutes. Turn legs; brush with sauce. Cook 5 to 10 minutes longer.

Teriyaki Chicken

> 2 chickens, cut up
> 1/4 cup sherry wine
> 2/3 cup soy sauce
> 1 clove garlic, chopped
> 3 tablespoons sugar
> 1/2 teaspoon ginger

Mix all ingredients together. Marinate chicken for 1 to 6 hours; the longer the chicken is marinated, the stronger the flavor. Bake at 325° for 1 1/2 hours.

Chicken Breast Supreme

> 6 chicken breasts, boned
> 6 slices of bacon
> 1 package of dried beef
> 1 can cream of mushroom soup
> 1 cup sour cream

Wrap boned chicken in bacon slices. Line a casserole with dried beef slices. Place chicken in casserole. Combine mushroom soup and sour cream. Pour over chicken and bake at 325° for 1 1/2 hours, or until tender.

California Chicken

You might want to ask the chicken for some identification, to make sure that it's from California...

> 8   boned chicken breasts
>   Seasoning salt and pepper to taste
> 2   cloves garlic, crushed
> 4   tablespoons olive oil
> 4   tablespoons tarragon vinegar
> 2/3   cup dry sherry

Sprinkle chicken with seasoning salt and pepper. Crush garlic into oil and vinegar in a frying pan. Sauté chicken pieces until golden brown, turning frequently. Remove and place chicken in a baking dish. Pour sherry over pieces and place in oven at 350° for 10 minutes.

Chicken Enchilada Casserole

> 4   chicken breasts
> 1   dozen corn tortillas
> 1   can cream mushroom soup
> 1   can cream chicken soup
> 1   cup milk
> 1   medium onion, grated
> 2   cans green chili salsa
> 1/2   pound Cheddar cheese, grated

Wrap chicken breasts in foil and bake at 400° for 1 hour. Bone and cut into large pieces.

Cut tortillas into small squares. Mix soups, milk, onion and salsa together. Butter large shallow baking dish and put 1 tablespoon juice from chicken in bottom. Place layer of tortillas, chicken and soup mixture in the baking dish; continue, ending with the soup mixture. Sprinkle with grated Cheddar cheese. Let stand 24 hours in refrigerator to blend flavors.

Cover with foil and bake at 300° for 1 1/2 hours.

Chicken and Broccoli Casserole

- 1 **4-pound chicken, roasted or boiled**
- 1 **bunch broccoli**
- 4 **tablespoons butter**
- 4 **tablespoons flour**
- 1 **teaspoon salt**
- 1/4 **teaspoon pepper**
- 4 **tablespoons Marsala wine**
- 1/4 **cup grated Parmesan cheese**
- 1/2 **cup whipping cream, whipped**

Cut the chicken into slices after it has cooled. Lay down a single layer of broccoli on bottom of casserole with a layer of sliced chicken.

Make sauce by blending butter with flour, salt, pepper, wine; fold in cheese and cream last. Cover broccoli and chicken with sauce. Bake at 350° for 25 minutes or until thoroughly heated.

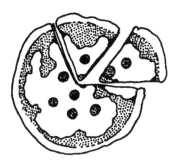

Pizza

- **French bread**
- 2/3 **cup Parmesan cheese, grated**
- 1 **cup mayonnaise**
- 1/4 **cup green onion, chopped**
- **Sausage, thinly sliced**

Slice French bread into 1-inch thick slices. Combine cheese, mayonnaise and green onions together. Spread mixture on bread slices. Spread on sausage slices. Bake at 350° for 15 minutes.

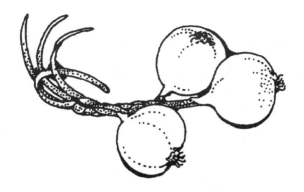

French Onion Soufflé

10	slices of French bread
8	tablespoons butter
1	cup onions, finely chopped
3	tablespoons flour
1 1/2	cups beef broth
	Salt and pepper to taste
6	egg yolks
8	egg whites, beaten
	Pinch of salt
1/8	teaspoon cream of tartar
1/2	cup Parmesan cheese, finely grated

Brush the sliced French bread with 4 tablespoons melted butter; crispen in the oven at 350° for 15 minutes.

Melt 4 tablespoons butter and add finely chopped onions. Sauté the onions in butter until soft and translucent. Add the flour. Gradually add the beef stock, stirring constantly to form a thick sauce. Season with salt and pepper. Remove the pan from the heat and add the egg yolks one at a time. Beat the egg whites until stiff, adding a pinch of salt and the cream of tartar. Fold in the beaten egg whites.

Cover the base of the prepared soufflé dish with rounds of lightly toasted French bread. Fill the soufflé mixture on top of the bread. Place rounds of French bread on top of the soufflé and sprinkle with Parmesan cheese. Bake at 375° for 25 minutes.

Crab and Noodle Casserole

1   package fine noodles, cooked
2   pounds crab meat
2   cans mushroom soup
5   tablespoons dry vermouth
2   teaspoons Worcestershire sauce
2   dashes cayenne pepper
2   dashes nutmeg
2   dashes garlic salt
2   dashes onion salt

Cook noodles. Drain and toss with remaining ingredients. Place in buttered casserole and bake at 350° until bubbly.

Crab-Stuffed Avocados

2   avocados
    Lemon juice
    Salt to taste
1   cup celery, diced
1   cup crab meat
1/2   cup mayonnaise

Cut the avocados lengthwise into halves, and remove the seeds. Sprinkle with lemon juice and salt. Combine celery and crab meat with the mayonnaise. Stuff the avocado halves with mixture and serve.

Scallops and Mushrooms

3   tablespoons butter
1   clove garlic, minced
1   pound medium scallops
1/2   pound mushrooms, sliced
1/2   cup green onions, chopped
1/4   cup white wine

Sauté garlic in butter over medium heat. Add scallops, mushrooms and green onions; sauté 3 minutes while stirring. Add white wine and cook 2 minutes more, or until scallops are ready. Serve with lemon slices.

Barbecued Salmon

If you like salmon, you'll <u>loooooove</u> this one!

6	**pound whole salmon**
1/4	**pound butter, melted**
1/4	**cup olive oil**
4	**garlic cloves, crushed**
1 1/2	**teaspoons Worcestershire sauce**
1	**teaspoon onion salt**
2	**dashes Tabasco sauce**
	Juice of 1/2 lemon
1/4	**cup dry white wine**
1	**tablespoon stone-ground mustard**
4	**tablespoons honey**

Make sauce by combining all of the ingredients, except the honey and salmon.

Clean salmon. Split open belly to dorsal fin; do not split down backbone. Lay the "butterflied" salmon skin side down on a medium-hot, greased barbecue grill. Puncture salmon in several places with fork. Sprinkle with freshly ground pepper. Brush prepared sauce on fish and close barbecue lid. Brush on sauce every 5 minutes. Salmon is ready when it flakes easily, about 20 to 30 minutes. During last 5 minutes, brush honey on fish to glaze.

Vegetables
&
Side Dishes

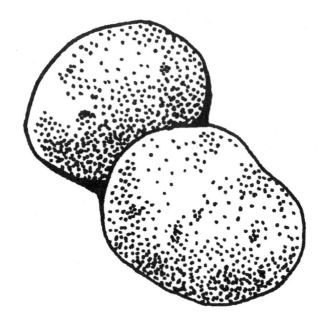

Old-Fashioned Mashed Potatoes

9   **large baking potatoes, peeled and diced**
1/2   **cup butter, room temperature**
12   **ounces cream cheese, room temperature**
3/4   **cup sour cream**
1/2   **teaspoon ground nutmeg**
        Salt to taste
        Ground black pepper to taste

Place diced potatoes in a large saucepan and cover with water. Heat to boiling. Reduce heat and simmer over medium heat until tender. Drain. Place the potatoes into a bowl.

Cut the butter and cream cheese into small pieces and add to the potatoes. Beat with a mixer until light and fluffy. Beat in the sour cream. Season with the nutmeg, salt and pepper. Serve mashed potatoes immediately, or reheat in a buttered casserole at 300° for about 20 minutes.

Baked Stuffed Potatoes

Go ahead and smother these taters with sour cream!

> **8** **medium potatoes**
> **Salt and pepper to taste**
> **Butter**
> **Milk**
> **1/2** **cup American cheese, grated**
> **Chives**
> **Paprika**

Scrub potatoes and bake until done.

Slice off the top and scoop out potato from skin, being very careful not to break the skin. Mash the potatoes with salt, pepper, butter and milk as required, until a proper consistency is reached. Add cheese to mixture.

Scoop the mashed mixture into potato skin shells. Sprinkle chives and paprika on top, and return to the oven at 300° for about 15 to 20 minutes.

Potatoes Parmesan

> **6** **medium-sized potatoes**
> **4** **tablespoons butter**
> **1/4** **cup beef broth**
> **1** **teaspoon salt**
> **1/2** **teaspoon black pepper**
> **1/2** **cup Parmesan cheese, grated**

Peel the potatoes and dice finely. Sauté in 2 tablespoons butter in a heavy frying pan for about 7 minutes, or until just tender. Add broth, salt and pepper.

Place potatoes in a greased shallow baking dish. Dot with the remaining butter and sprinkle with Parmesan cheese. Bake at 400° until browned, about 35 minutes.

Glazed Sweet Potatoes

No, a sweet potato is not the same as a yam. However, you never really seem to see the two in the same place, at the same time, now do you?

> **6**   **sweet potatoes**
> **1**   **cup brown sugar**
> **1/4** **cup water**
>   **Butter**
>   **Salt and pepper to taste**

Boil potatoes without paring them. When potatoes are tender, drain and remove skins.

Combine brown sugar and water into a thick syrup. Cut potatoes in half, dip into the syrup and place in baking dish. Season with salt, pepper and a little butter. Bake at 450° until potatoes are brown.

Yams

No, a yam is not the same as a sweet potato. So, what is the difference? Well, if you asked a yam, he would probably just wink and say, "I yam what I yam."

> **6**   **yams**
> **1**   **cup brown sugar**
> **1/4** **cup water**
> **4**   **tablespoons butter**
>   **Salt and pepper to taste**

Boil yams without paring them. When yams are tender, drain and remove skins.

Cook brown sugar and water over medium heat, stirring constantly until it thickens. Slice yams in thick slices and lay in greased pan. Spread with butter. Pour syrup over yams. Season with salt and pepper. Bake uncovered at 350° for about 1 hour, until transparent.

Baked Beans

2   1-pound cans baked beans
1   large onion, thinly sliced

Sauce:

1   cup catsup
1 1/2   tablespoons Worcestershire sauce
4   tablespoons brown sugar
4   tablespoons lemon juice
1   teaspoon dry mustard
    Dash of Tabasco sauce

Combine all sauce ingredients.

Empty 1 can of beans in large casserole. Cover beans with half the onion slices and half of the sauce. Add second can of beans and cover with remaining onion slices and sauce. Cover and bake in oven at 300° for 3 hours.

Refried Beans

1 1/2   cups onion, chopped
2   tomatoes, chopped
3   tablespoons vegetable oil
4   1-pound cans refried beans
1/2   cup beer
    Salt and pepper to taste
2   cups sharp Cheddar cheese, shredded

In a large frying pan, sauté onion and tomatoes in oil until tender, but not brown. Stir in beans and beer. Cook uncovered while stirring occasionally, until mixture has thickened and will not run when spooned onto a plate. Season to taste with salt and pepper. Stir in 1 cup of cheese. Place mixture in a 7x11-inch baking dish. Top with remaining cheese. Refrigerate or freeze.

Before reheating, bring beans to room temperature. Bake in oven at 400° for 30 minutes, until bubbly. Cool before serving.

String Beans

1   **pound string beans, cooked and drained**
1   **cucumber, diced**
2   **green onions, chopped**
    Salt and pepper to taste
    Mayonnaise

Add to hot string beans a diced cucumber and green onions. Season with salt and pepper to taste. Toss with mayonnaise. Serve warm, but do not cook after mixing.

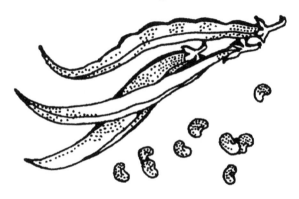

Green Beans

4   **cups green beans, cut**
2   **cups celery, sliced diagonally**
1/2 **cup onion, chopped**
2   **tablespoons margarine**
1   **cup Thousand Island dressing**
4   **hard-boiled eggs, sliced**
8   **strips cooked bacon, crumbled**

Cook celery and onion in margarine until crisp-tender. Add green beans, heating thoroughly. Add dressing and half of the eggs and bacon; heat. Place in a dish. Sprinkle remaining eggs and bacon over the top.

Bean Sprouts

2	tablespoons oil
1/4	cup water
4	tablespoons onion, shredded
2	tablespoons green pepper, thinly sliced
1/2	pound bean sprouts
	Soy sauce to taste
	Dash of salt

Place oil and water in frying pan and heat. Add onion and green pepper, stirring until onion is tender. Add bean sprouts, soy sauce and salt. Cover and cook for 5 minutes.

French Green Peas

2	cups fresh green peas, shelled
2	tablespoons butter
12	small white onions
1	stalk parsley
1/4	teaspoon sugar
1/2	teaspoon salt
1/4	teaspoon dried chervil
1/4	cup boiling water
4	lettuce leaves, shredded
1	teaspoon flour
1/8	teaspoon ground black pepper

Wash peas and place them in a saucepan with 1 tablespoon of butter and the next 6 ingredients. Arrange the shredded lettuce over the peas. Cover and cook over medium heat until about 2 or 3 tablespoons of water is left in the pan, about 25 to 30 minutes.

Blend flour with 1 tablespoon butter and add to peas. Shake the pan over the heat to blend the mixture with the pan liquid; but do not stir. Remove the peas from the heat when they begin to boil. Remove parsley stalk. Add pepper and serve immediately.

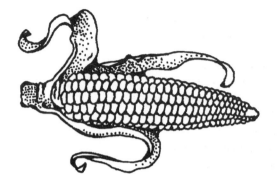

Western-Style Corn on the Cob

1/2   **cup soft butter**
1   **tablespoon prepared mustard**
1   **teaspoon prepared horseradish**
1   **teaspoon salt**
  Dash freshly ground pepper
4   **ears sweet corn**
  Parsley, snipped

Prepare horseradish butter by combining the butter, mustard, horseradish, salt and pepper. Cream until light and fluffy.

Husk corn and strip off the silk. Spread each ear with a little horseradish butter. Wrap each loosely in foil and bake at 450° for 20 to 25 minutes. Combine butter with parsley spread on corn.

Spanish Corn

2   **packages frozen corn**
1   **green pepper, diced**
1/2   **cup pimento, drained and diced**
  Butter
  Salt and white pepper to taste

Cook the corn. In a separate pan, boil the green pepper for a short time. Add the green pepper and the pimento, after draining and buttering the corn. Season with salt and white pepper.

German Spinach

1 1/2	pounds fresh spinach
2	tablespoons butter
1	small onion, finely chopped
1	tablespoon flour
3/4	cup milk
	Salt and pepper to taste
1/8	teaspoon garlic salt

Wash spinach in cold water, lifting leaves from the water instead of pouring water off. Remove thick stems. Cook in 1 cup of boiling water in a covered saucepan for 6 to 7 minutes. Drain.

Cook onion in butter until transparent. Add flour and blend. Add milk. Cook and stir until thickened. Add chopped spinach, salt, pepper and garlic salt. Heat to serving temperature.

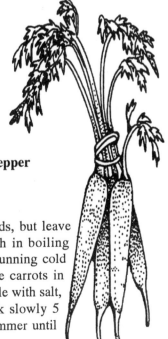

Creamed Carrots

1	pound tender carrots
3	tablespoons butter
	Salt and ground black pepper
1/2	teaspoon sugar
1/3	cup heavy cream

Wash carrots and trim both ends, but leave them whole with skins on. Blanch in boiling water for 5 minutes; rinse under running cold water. Slip off the skins. Sauté the carrots in butter in a heavy frying pan. Sprinkle with salt, pepper and sugar. Cover and cook slowly 5 minutes. Add cream. Cover and simmer until carrots are tender.

Brussels Sprouts

4 cups brussels sprouts, trimmed
1 stalk celery, coarsely chopped
Salt to taste
Freshly ground pepper to taste
6 tablespoons butter, melted
1/2 cup Gruyére cheese, grated
1/4 cup Parmesan cheese, grated

Score the bottoms of brussels sprouts. Steam sprouts and celery until just tender; set aside.

Sprinkle a buttered shallow baking dish with salt and pepper. Coat bottom of dish with 4 tablespoons of the melted butter. Heat in the oven at 350° for 5 minutes.

Reset oven to 425°. Combine cheeses. Layer brussels sprouts and celery with cheeses in the baking dish, finishing with a layer of cheese. Sprinkle 2 tablespoons butter over all and bake 10 minutes, or until cheese is melted and vegetables are warm.

Glazed Onions

2 pounds small white onions
1 cup beef bouillon
1 tablespoon sugar
2 tablespoons prepared mustard
1/2 teaspoon salt
1/4 teaspoon paprika
1/3 cup butter, melted

Peel onions and cut shallow crosses in the stem end. Combine with bouillon in a saucepan. Bring to a boil. Cover and simmer until tender, about 20 to 30 minutes. Drain. Place onions in shallow baking dish.

Combine sugar, mustard, salt, paprika and melted butter. Mix well and pour over onions. Bake at 350° for 20 minutes, basting and turning occasionally.

Artichokes

4   large artichokes, chilled
1   bay leaf, crushed
4   pinches basil
**   Garlic, minced**
**   Salt to taste**

Cut off tips from each artichoke. Tuck into each artichoke 1/4 crushed bay leaf, a pinch of basil, and bits of minced garlic. Put petal end down into 1/2 cup boiling water. Cover and steam for 20 to 30 minutes, or until tender. Drain. Sprinkle artichokes with salt. Serve hot with melted butter, or chilled with mayonnaise.

Zucchini

4   zucchini, sliced
**   Butter**
1   small onion, finely chopped
**   Garlic salt and Italian herbs to taste**

Sauté chopped onion in butter. When onion begins to brown, add sliced zucchini. Sauté until tender-crisp, stirring several times. Sprinkle on garlic salt and Italian herbs to taste.

Latvian Sauerkraut

An old Latvian favorite that is the <u>best</u>!

> 2   **28-ounce large cans sauerkraut**
> 1   **head cabbage, shredded**
> 1   **large onion, chopped**
> 1/2 **pound bacon, chopped**
> 1   **cup sugar**
> 2   **tablespoons caraway seeds**

Place the sauerkraut into a large pot. Add the cabbage, onions, bacon, sugar and caraway seeds. Add water to just barely cover the sauerkraut. Bring to boil; then lower heat and simmer covered for 4 to 5 hours, stirring occasionally. Add more sugar if needed, while sauerkraut is cooking, tasting often. Near the end of cooking, after about 3 to 4 hours, uncover pot to boil off any excess water as required. The sauerkraut should taste sweet-sour, but not too sweet.

Sauerkraut tastes better the more it's reheated, so it's better to cook it a day before serving.

Wild Rice

> 2   **eggs**
> 2/3 **cup olive oil**
> 1   **onion, finely chopped**
> 1   **cup parsley, chopped**
> 2   **cups Eastern cheese, grated**
> 2   **cups wild rice, boiled dry**
> 1   **cup milk**
>   **Salt and pepper to taste**

Beat eggs well. Add oil slowly, then onion, parsley and 1/2 cup cheese. Mix all together well. Add cooked rice and 1 cup milk. Salt and pepper to taste. Put in casserole and sprinkle cheese on top. Cook in oven at 350° for 30 minutes or more.

Green Rice

> 5 cups steamed rice
> 2 large sprigs parsley, finely chopped
> 4 green onions, finely chopped
> 1 Lump of butter

Cook the rice. Add parsley and onions. Place in casserole with lump of butter, and warm for 10 minutes. Mix lightly with fork before serving.

Confetti Rice

> 1/2 cup onions, chopped
> 1/2 cup green pepper, diced
> 6 tablespoons butter
> 12 medium-sized mushrooms, sliced
> 3 cups rice, cooked
> 1/2 teaspoon salt
> 1/2 teaspoon fines herbs
> 1/4 teaspoon pepper
> 3 tablespoons parsley, finely chopped
> 2 tablespoons pimento, chopped

Butter a 1 1/2-quart baking dish. Sauté onions and green pepper in butter until almost tender. Add mushrooms and cook until mushrooms are just tender. Combine with remaining ingredients and seasonings. Place in buttered baking dish. Cover and bake at 350° for 30 minutes, or until thoroughly heated.

Brown Rice

- 1   cup brown rice, uncooked
- 1   4-ounce can French fried onions
- 1   2-ounce can mushroom stems and pieces
- 1/4 cup stuffed green olives, sliced
- 2   cans mushroom soup
- 1/2 cup milk
- 1/4 teaspoon pepper
- 1/4 cup Parmesan cheese, grated

Cook brown rice by the instructions on box. Drain and place in a 2-quart casserole. Add the onions, mushrooms (save the mushroom juice for later), and olives to rice; mix all gently.

In another bowl, mix together the mushroom soup, milk, pepper and juice saved from the mushrooms; set aside mixture.

When ready to bake, pour the mushroom soup mixture into the rice mixture, mixing all gently. Bake uncovered at 350° for 30 minutes. Sprinkle Parmesan cheese over the top and bake for 10 more minutes.

Rice-Stuffed Tomatoes

- 6   fresh tomatoes
- 3   tablespoons brown sugar
-     Salt to taste
- 1/4 pound mushrooms, sliced
-     Butter
- 1/2 cup rice, cooked
- 1/2 cup sharp Cheddar cheese, grated

Scoop out tomatoes. Season each shell with brown sugar and salt. Sauté mushrooms in butter. Mix rice and mushrooms. Fill tomato shells with rice mixture. Sprinkle top with cheese. Place tomato shells in a pan with enough water to keep them from scorching. Bake at 350° for 10 to 15 minutes. Before serving, place under broiler for a few minutes to brown.

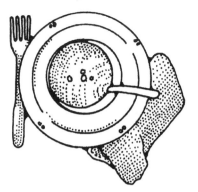

Cream of Green Pea Soup

2   **10-ounce packages frozen green peas**
1   **small onion, sliced**
2   **cups chicken broth**
4   **tablespoons butter**
2   **cups milk**
1 1/2   **cups cream**
     Salt and pepper to taste

Cook peas and onion in chicken broth. Blend mixture in blender until smooth. Stir in butter, milk and cream. Heat soup until boiling. Add salt and pepper to taste.

Avocado Soup

1   **avocado**
1   **can jellied consommé**
1   **tablespoon lemon juice**
     Salt and pepper to taste
     Sour cream
     Avocado, diced (for garnish)

Peel avocado and put into blender with consommé, lemon juice, salt and pepper. Blend well until smooth. Chill in refrigerator. Pour into individual bowls. Top each bowl of soup with 1 teaspoon sour cream, and diced avocado. Serve cold.

Crab Soup

1/2	pound crab meat
2	cans tomato soup
1	can split pea soup
1	can beef broth
1/2	cup sherry
1/2	cup half and half cream

Mix together tomato soup, split pea soup, beef broth and sherry; heat to boiling. Add half and half cream; return to boiling. Fold in crab meat. Pour into individual bowls and serve.

Vegetable Casserole

1	pound zucchini, sliced
1	package baby lima beans, frozen
1/2	pound mushrooms
1	can mushroom soup
1/2	cup cashew nuts, chopped
	Butter

Butter a casserole. Arrange uncooked zucchini, lima beans and mushrooms in layers. Pour mushroom soup over all. Bake at 350° for 50 minutes. Add cashew nuts and bits of butter. Bake 10 minutes more.

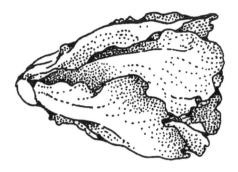

Cheese and Spinach Soufflé

1	pound cottage cheese, creamed
3	eggs
1/4	cup butter, cubed
1/4	pound Cheddar cheese, cubed
1	package frozen spinach, thawed and chopped
3	tablespoons flour

Place cottage cheese in a bowl. Add eggs and mix. Add butter and Cheddar cheese. Drain spinach and add to cheese mixture, mixing well. Add flour and mix until blended well. Pour into a lightly greased 1 1/2 quart casserole. Bake uncovered at 350° for 1 hour.

German Potato Pancakes

4	medium raw potatoes, grated
1	cup mashed potatoes, cooked
1	egg yolk
1	egg
1	teaspoon salt
1/2	teaspoon pepper

Drain raw grated potatoes. Combine grated potatoes with mashed potatoes, egg yolk, egg, salt and pepper. Form into pancakes. Fry in butter until brown and crispy.

Hominy Grits

The favorite dish among 4 out of 5 barbershop quartets...

     1   **quart milk**
     1   **cup hominy grits**
     1   **cup butter**
     1   **teaspoon salt**
     1   **teaspoon pepper**
   1/2   **cup butter, melted**
     1   **cup Gruyére cheese, shredded**
   1/2   **cup Parmesan cheese**

Pour milk into a double boiler. Add hominy grits and 1 cup butter. Cook until thick. Remove from heat and add salt and pepper. Pour into a buttered 8x11-inch baking dish. Pour 1/2 cup melted butter over this, followed by Gruyére cheese and Parmesan cheese. Bake at 350° for 30 minutes, or until light brown.

Noodles with Basil

     1   **12-ounce package egg noodles**
     1   **8-ounce package cream cheese**
     1   **small can black olives, chopped and drained**
   1/4   **cup butter**
 1 1/2   **teaspoons dried basil**
         Salt to taste
         Freshly ground pepper to taste

Cook noodles; drain and keep hot. Soften cream cheese and stir in olives. Stir cream cheese mixture into the hot noodles, stirring until cheese has completely melted. Melt butter; add basil, salt and pepper to taste. Stir butter mixture into noodles. Place in a 2-quart casserole and bake at 325° for 20 to 30 minutes.

Noodles Romanoff

1   6-ounce package noodles, cooked and drained
1   cup cottage cheese
1   teaspoon salt
1   cup sour cream
1/4   cup parsley, chopped
1/4   cup onions, chopped
2   teaspoons Worcestershire sauce
3   drops Tabasco sauce
    Parmesan cheese, grated

Mix together all ingredients well, except noodles and cheese. Fold mixture into noodles. Pour into a greased casserole. Sprinkle with grated cheese to cover. Bake at 350° for 35 minutes, or until thoroughly heated.

Breads

Applesauce Oatmeal Bread

1 1/2	cups all-purpose flour
1	teaspoon baking powder
1	teaspoon baking soda
1	teaspoon salt
1	teaspoon cinnamon
1/2	teaspoon nutmeg
1	cup rolled oats
1/2	cup raisins
1/2	cup shortening
1/2	cup brown sugar
2	eggs
1	cup apple sauce, unsweetened
1/2	cup milk

Preheat oven to 350°. Grease well a 9x5x3-inch loaf pan. Sift together flour, baking powder, baking soda, salt, cinnamon and nutmeg. Stir in rolled oats and raisins.

Cream shortening and brown sugar together. Add eggs, beat until light and fluffy. Blend in applesauce and milk. Add dry ingredients and beat about 30 seconds; batter may be lumpy. Turn into loaf pan.

Bake in preheated 350° oven for 50 to 60 minutes, or until a toothpick inserted comes out clean.

Peanut Butter Bread

- 2 cups all-purpose flour
- 1/3 cup sugar
- 1 teaspoon salt
- 2 teaspoons baking powder
- 3/4 cup peanut butter
- 1 egg, beaten
- 1 cup milk, scant

Sift together flour, sugar, salt and baking powder. Add peanut butter and egg to dry ingredients. Add milk. Pour into buttered loaf pan. Bake at 350° for 50 to 60 minutes.

Banana Nut Bread

- 2 2/3 cups sifted all-purpose flour
- 3 teaspoons baking powder
- 1 teaspoon salt
- 1/4 teaspoon baking soda
- 1/2 cup butter
- 1 cup sugar
- 3 eggs
- 2 medium-size ripe bananas, mashed
- 2 teaspoons orange rind, grated
- 3/4 cup pecans, finely chopped

Grease a 9x5x3-inch loaf pan. Line bottom of pan with wax paper; grease the wax paper.

Sift flour, baking powder, salt and baking soda onto a wax paper sheet. In a bowl, cream butter with sugar, until light and fluffy. Beat in eggs, one by one, until fluffy. Stir in flour mixture, alternately with mashed bananas; fold in orange rind and pecans.

Pour into loaf pan. Bake at 325° for 1 hour and 20 minutes, or until golden and a toothpick comes out clean. Cool in pan 15 minutes. Loosen around edges and turn bread out of pan. Remove waxed paper. Allow to cool. Wrap bread and store overnight.

Cranberry Bread

      2 **cups flour**
      1 **cup sugar**
1 1/2 **teaspoons baking powder**
   1/2 **teaspoon soda**
   1/2 **teaspoon salt**
      1 **egg, beaten**
      2 **tablespoons shortening, melted**
   1/2 **cup orange juice**
      2 **tablespoons hot water**
      1 **cup fresh cranberries, chopped**
   1/2 **cup nuts**

Sift together flour, sugar, baking powder, soda and salt. Add beaten egg, shortening, orange juice and hot water. Combine until dry ingredients are moistened. Fold in cranberries and nuts. Pour into loaf pan.

Bake at 325° for 1 hour and 10 minutes. Allow to cool in refrigerator for 24 hours before serving.

Garlic Bread

So good, you won't care about bad breath...

      1 **loaf French bread**
          Butter
          Garlic, chopped
          Dash of onion salt

Slice the French bread loaf almost through, making thick slices. Place butter liberally between slices. Spread slices apart and sprinkle in chopped garlic and a dash of onion salt. Place in 400° oven and heat.

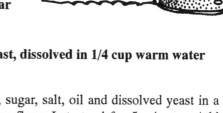

French Bread

      2 1/2   **cups warm water**
          1   **tablespoon sugar**
          1   **tablespoon salt**
          1   **tablespoon oil**
          2   **tablespoons yeast, dissolved in 1/4 cup warm water**
          2   **cups flour**

Combine warm water, sugar, salt, oil and dissolved yeast in a large bowl. Beat in 2 cups flour. Let stand for 5 minutes. Add more flour until dough is fairly stiff. Let dough rise until doubled. Form 2 long loaves and place on greased cookie sheet. Allow dough to rise.

Bake at 350° for 45 to 60 minutes. After 20 minutes, sprinkle water on loaves every 10 minutes for a browner crust.

Corn Bread

          1   **cup sifted all-purpose flour**
          1   **teaspoon salt**
          1   **tablespoon baking powder**
          4   **tablespoons sugar**
        3/4   **cup yellow corn meal**
          2   **eggs**
          1   **cup milk**
        1/4   **cup melted butter**

Sift flour, salt, baking powder and sugar together. Add corn meal and mix well. Beat the eggs until light and fluffy; mix with milk and butter. Add liquid mixture to dry ingredients all at once. Blend using only a few strokes, do not beat. Pour into a well-greased 8-inch square pan.

Place into 400° oven for about 30 minutes, or when toothpick inserted comes out clean. Serve corn bread warm with butter.

Rye Bread

Warm it up, spread on lots of butter, and it melts in your mouth!

        8   cups rye flour
        2   tablespoons caraway seeds
       12   cups water
        1   cup starter dough (from a previous baking or made
            from the recipe below)

        3   envelopes dry yeast
      3/4   cup warm water
        1   teaspoon sugar

        3   cups sugar
        1   teaspoon salt
       20   cups white all-purpose flour
        1   piece of bacon

Rye Bread Starter Dough:

        1   cup rye flour
        2   cups warm water
        1   tablespoon dry yeast
      1/4   cup yogurt, made with a natural culture

Mix all starter dough ingredients together and place in a glass jar; cover, without sealing. Put in a warm place and allow to ferment for 3 days. Then, seal and refrigerate.

Rye Bread:

Put rye flour in a 12-quart pot. Add caraway seeds to 12 cups water. Heat water to near boiling; not boiling. Pour water over rye flour and mix with a wooden spoon or mixer until smooth.

When mixture has cooled to lukewarm, add starter dough. Stir well. Sprinkle a thick layer of rye flour on top. Cover with heavy blankets and let rise overnight in a warm place.

The next day, in a small bowl, mix dry yeast with 3/4 cup warm water and 1 teaspoon sugar. When yeast has risen, mix it into the dough. Add 3 cups sugar and 1 teaspoon salt to dough.

Stir well. Gradually, add white flour while kneading well. Allow dough to rise in a warm place until it doubles in size.

Divide dough into 6 well-greased loaf pans, only 3/4 full. Allow dough to rise again to fill pans.

Preheat oven to 375°. Bake for 1 to 1 1/4 hours, until a toothpick inserted into bread comes out clean.

Remove loaves from pans and place on a rack. Brush tops of loaves with a piece of bacon to make shiny. Cover loaves with a towel and allow to cool.

Rye bread will mold easily, so keep the loaf you are eating wrapped in aluminum foil and inside a plastic bag; store in the refrigerator. Wrap the other loaves in aluminum foil and plastic bags after they have cooled; store loaves in the freezer. The rye bread will stay fresh and delicious.

Warm sliced bread in oven or microwave before serving. Serve with butter, peanut butter or cottage cheese.

Save some dough to use as a starter next time. Keep it in the freezer, and thaw before using.

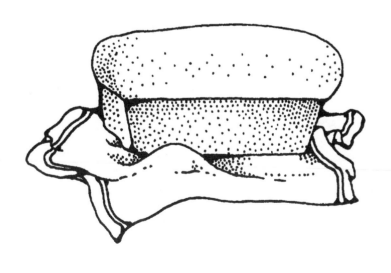

Water Pretzels

These are not the hard pretzels that you may be thinking of, they are delicious soft bagels that are shaped like pretzels.

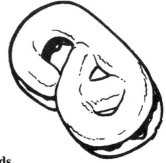

1 1/2	**cups water**
1	**teaspoon sugar**
2	**tablespoons dry yeast**
7 - 8	**cups all-purpose flour**
1/4	**cup butter**
2	**cups water**
3	**tablespoons sugar**
1	**tablespoon salt**
1	**tablespoon caraway seeds**

Place 1 1/2 cups warm water in a large bowl; add 1 teaspoon sugar and sprinkle in yeast. Let stand 10 minutes. Beat in 2 cups flour. Allow to rise 30 minutes.

Melt the butter in 2 cups of hot water. Add 3 tablespoons sugar, 1 tablespoon salt and caraway seeds. Cool to lukewarm.

Add 4 cups flour to the yeast mixture; pour butter mixture over it and beat using a wooden spoon until the dough forms into a soft ball.

Turn dough onto a floured board. Knead and add more flour until dough is elastic and firm. Place in bowl; let rise 1 hour. Punch dough down and knead awhile to deflate. Divide dough into 36 pieces. Roll each piece to make a long enough strand to form a large, palm-sized pretzel. Moisten the ends, twist and press them to the back of the pretzel. Let them relax until all are shaped.

In a large saucepan, bring 2 quarts of water, 1 1/2 tablespoons salt, and 1 tablespoon sugar to boil. Drop 2 to 3 pretzels in at a time, without crowding. Boil each 15 seconds, turn over and boil 15 seconds more. Remove with slotted spoon and place onto paper towels to drain.

Place pretzels on greased baking sheets. Bake at 425° for 15 to 20 minutes, until tops are brown. Serve warm with butter, peanut butter or cream cheese.

Yorkshire Pudding

1 3/4 **cups sifted all-purpose flour**
1 **teaspoon salt**
1 **cup milk**
4 **eggs**
1 **cup water**
1/2 **cube butter**

Sift flour and salt into a bowl. Make a well in the center and pour in milk; stir in the milk. Beat eggs into batter; add water. Beat the batter until smooth.

Put butter into a 9x13-inch pan. Place in a 400° oven. When the butter sizzles, pour batter in and bake for 20 minutes. Reduce heat to 350° and bake for 10 to 15 minutes longer, until pudding is brown and puffy. Serve when hot.

Corn Pudding

6 **tablespoons butter, melted**
3/4 **cup corn meal**
2 **teaspoons baking powder**
1/2 **teaspoon salt**
1 **cup boiling water**
2 **cups scalding milk**
3 **eggs, beaten**
1 **can cream of corn**

Melt 2 tablespoons butter in a casserole. Mix the corn meal with the baking powder and salt. Then, add the rest of the butter. Scald mixture with 1 cup boiling water; beat the mixture. Add scalding milk and beaten eggs; beat well. Stir in corn.

Bake at 375° for 35 to 40 minutes, until pudding is puffed up and golden brown.

Blueberry Muffins

2	cups sifted flour
3	teaspoons double-acting baking powder
3	tablespoons sugar
1/4	teaspoon salt
3/4	teaspoon cinnamon
3/4	cup milk
1	egg, well beaten
1/2	cup butter, melted
1	cup blueberries

Sift flour and measure 2 cups. Combine the sifted flour with baking powder, sugar, salt and cinnamon; sift again. Combine the milk and beaten egg; mix with the dry ingredients. Add melted butter and blend thoroughly. Fold in blueberries. Butter muffin tins and fill each 2/3 full of batter.

Bake at 400° for about 25 minutes, or until muffins are brown, puffy and done through.

Lemon Muffins

    2 lemons
    1 cup flour
    1 teaspoon baking powder
  1/4 teaspoon salt
  1/2 cup butter
  1/2 cup and 2 tablespoons sugar
    2 eggs, separated
  1/4 teaspoon cinnamon

Grate rind off lemons. Squeeze 3 tablespoons juice; set aside.

Sift together flour, baking powder and salt. Cream butter with 1/2 cup sugar until light and fluffy. Beat in egg yolks one at a time. Add flour mixture alternately with lemon juice; do not overmix. Beat whites until stiff but not dry, and fold with grated rind into batter. Fill lightly greased muffin tins 3/4 full.

Combine remaining sugar and cinnamon, and sprinkle over muffins. Bake in preheated 375° oven 25 minutes or until done.

English Muffins

      1 cup flour
      1 cup corn meal
      3 tablespoons sugar
      4 teaspoons baking powder
      1 teaspoon salt
      2 eggs
  1 1/4 cups milk
      3 tablespoons shortening, melted

Mix together flour, corn meal, sugar, baking powder and salt. Beat eggs; add to milk with melted shortening. Combine both mixtures. Pour into a greased muffin tin.

Bake at 350° for 30 minutes or until done. Serve hot with butter or favorite jelly.

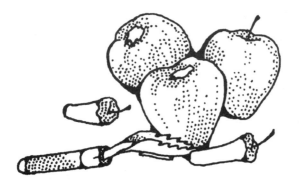

Apple Muffins

2	cups sifted all-purpose flour
1/2	cup sugar
3	teaspoons baking powder
1	teaspoon salt
1/2	cup butter
1	medium-size tart apple; pared, sliced and diced
2	teaspoons lemon rind, grated
1	egg
2/3	cup milk
1/4	cup walnuts, chopped
2	tablespoons sugar

Sift flour, 1/2 cup sugar, baking powder and salt into a large bowl. Cut in butter with a blender until mixture is crumbly. Measure out 1/2 cup for topping and set aside.

Stir apple and 1 teaspoon of the lemon rind into mixture in bowl. Beat egg in a small bowl; stir in milk. Add all at once to apple mixture and stir lightly just until moist; batter will be lumpy. Spoon into 12 greased medium muffin-pan cups, filling each only 2/3 full.

Blend reserved crumb mixture with remaining lemon rind, walnuts and 2 tablespoons sugar. Sprinkle over batter in each cup.

Bake at 425° for 20 minutes, or until golden and muffin tops feel springy. Remove muffins from cups. Serve with butter and jelly as desired.

French Toast

- **12 slices bread**
- **3 eggs**
- **2 cups milk**
- **1/2 teaspoon salt**
  Powdered sugar

Beat eggs; add milk and salt. Dip bread slices into mixture. Sauté slices in a little hot fat until light brown. Dust with powdered sugar. Serve hot with favorite syrup.

Popovers

- **1 cup sifted all-purpose flour**
- **1 cup milk**
- **1/4 teaspoon salt**
- **2 eggs**
- **1 tablespoon butter, melted**

Place muffin pans in a 350° oven. Mix flour and milk well; add salt. Beat in eggs one at a time; add melted butter. After muffin pans are hot, place 1 teaspoon of butter in each. Fill each pan 2/3 full of batter. Bake at 350° for 45 minutes or until done.

Cinnamon Rolls

1	package dry yeast
1/4	cup water, lukewarm
1/4	cup sugar
1	teaspoon salt
5	tablespoons shortening (1/2 butter)
3/4	cup scalded milk
1	egg, beaten
3 1/2	cups flour
	Butter
	Cinnamon
	Brown sugar

Dissolve yeast in 1/4 cup lukewarm water.

Mix the sugar, salt and shortening in a bowl; pour the scalded milk over them. While this is cooling, beat the egg and add to dissolved yeast. Add the yeast mixture to the lukewarm milk mixture. Add 1/2 cup flour and beat well; add the rest of the flour. Cover and put in refrigerator for about 1 hour.

Spread on floured board. Spread out using plenty of butter, cinnamon and sugar. Roll like a jelly roll, and cut into about 1/2 inch thick pinwheels.

In bottom of baking pan, melt butter and brown sugar. Place pinwheels into this; not too close together. Let rise for about 2 hours in a warm place (80° to 85°). The pinwheels should almost double in size. Bake at 400° for 12 to 15 minutes.

Danish Pastry

1/4	cup light brown sugar
1	cube butter
1	cup flour
1	egg
1	cup walnuts, crushed
	Jam or jelly of choice

Cream together butter and brown sugar. Add flour, mixing well with hands. Add egg yolk. Form mixture into walnut-sized balls. Dip into egg white, then roll in crushed walnuts. Place on a greased cookie sheet. Dent the middle deeply with finger.

Bake at 375° for 5 minutes, and then dent again with finger. Bake again until golden brown. Drop jam or jelly into depression.

Sour Cream Pancakes

- **1/2 cup sifted all-purpose flour**
- **1 tablespoon sugar**
- **1/2 teaspoon salt**
- **6 eggs, separated**
- **1 cup sour cream**

Sift flour; add sugar and salt. Beat egg whites until stiff. Beat egg yolks until thick. Mix egg yolks with sour cream; stir into flour mixture. Fold in egg whites, lightly but completely. Drop batter by small spoonfuls into a hot buttered frying pan. Brown on both sides. Serve with jam, or powdered sugar and lemon juice.

Apple Pancakes

- **5 apples, quartered and sliced thinly**
- **3 eggs, well beaten**
- **1 cup milk**
- **1/2 teaspoon salt**
- **Flour**

Combine eggs, milk and salt. Gradually add enough flour to make a smooth batter. Add apples to batter. Fry on a well-buttered fry pan until golden brown on each side, and apples are tender. Flip pancakes over only once. When done, sprinkle with sugar and cinnamon. Serve with butter and favorite syrup.

Swedish Pancakes

1	cup flour
1	teaspoon sugar
1/4	teaspoon salt
1	teaspoon baking powder
1 1/2	cups milk
1/2	cup half and half
3	eggs, separated
3/4	cube butter

Sift flour and add sugar, salt and baking powder. Add milk, and half and half. Add 3 beaten egg yolks. Add 3 whipped egg whites, fold into batter and add 3/4 cube melted butter. Drop batter by spoonfuls into a hot buttered frying pan. Brown on both sides.

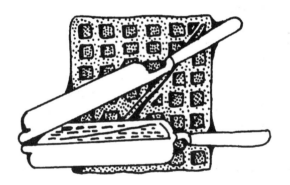

Buttermilk Waffles

Granny couldn't get these out of the waffle iron fast enough to keep up with the folks devouring them at the breakfast table...

3	eggs, separated
1	cup buttermilk
2	tablespoons butter, melted
1	cup flour
1	teaspoon baking powder
1	tablespoon sugar

Whip egg whites until stiff. Beat egg yolks until lemon colored. Add buttermilk, melted butter, flour, baking powder and sugar to egg yolks; mix together. Fold in whipped egg whites.

Spray waffle iron with no-stick spray. Pour batter into hot waffle iron. Remove waffle when crisp and brown. Serve with melted butter, syrup or powdered sugar.

Golden Crêpes

Treat your family to this "mouth-watering" breakfast...

Batter:

8	eggs
1 1/4	cups flour
1 1/4	cups oil
1	cup milk
3/4	cup water
1/2	teaspoon salt
1	tablespoon sugar

Combine all ingredients. Mix well. Keep in refrigerator at least 8 hours. Pour very thin layer in a 8-inch frying pan. Brown very slightly on both sides. Fill with cottage cheese or other favorite filling.

Cottage Cheese Filling:

1	pound dry cottage cheese
1	large package cream cheese
1	lemon; juice and grated rind
1	cup sugar
4	eggs
1	teaspoon vanilla extract

Blend all ingredients in mixer. Spoon a large tablespoon in the center of pancake. Fold like an envelope. Brown in butter until golden on both sides. Serve hot with fruit sauce or preserve. Can be frozen and reheated.

Desserts

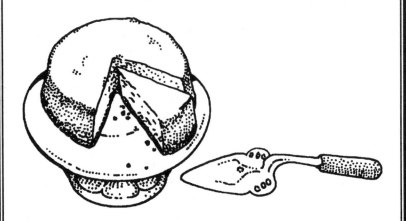

Cheese Cake

Moist and <u>incredibly</u> delicious!

2	tablespoons butter, room temperature
1 1/3	cups graham cracker crumbs
1 1/4	pounds cream cheese, room temperature
3/4	cup whipping cream
3	tablespoons lemon juice
2	teaspoons vanilla
3/4	cup sour cream
1 1/4	cups sugar
4	large eggs, slightly beaten, room temperature

Grease 8-inch spring-form pan evenly with butter. Place graham cracker crumbs in pan, shake pan to evenly coat bottom and sides with crumbs. Press crumbs gently into place. Turn pan over to remove any excess crumbs; set aside.

Cut cream cheese into 1-inch cubes; place in large mixer bowl. Beat at medium speed, scraping down sides of bowl as needed, until completely smooth. Continue beating while slowly adding whipping cream, lemon juice and vanilla, scraping down sides of bowl as required. Beat until mixture is smooth.

Add sour cream to cheese mixture; beat at a medium speed until blended. Continue beating the mixture while very slowly adding sugar; beat until sugar is blended in. Add eggs, a little at a time, beating well and scraping down the sides of the bowl after each addition.

Pour batter into pan. Gently rotate pan several turns to settle batter. Bake at 325° until sides of cake are set 2 inches in from edges and center is still pudding-like, about 1 hour and 15 minutes, for a creamy center. For a firmer center, bake until center is just set, 8 to 10 minutes longer. Turn oven off. Let cake sit in oven with door open 6 inches for 30 minutes.

Transfer pan to rack; allow to cool until bottom and sides of pan are completely cooled. Remove sides of pan. Refrigerate cake uncovered at least 8 hours or overnight; then cover cake loosely with plastic wrap. Refrigerate until serving.

Before serving, top with strawberries or other fruit.

Carrot Cake

- 3 **cups all-purpose flour**
- 2 **teaspoons baking powder**
- 1 **teaspoon baking soda**
- 1 **teaspoon cinnamon**
- 4 **eggs**
- 2 **cups sugar**
- 1 **cup salad oil**
- 2 **teaspoons vanilla flavor**
- 3 **cups carrots, grated**
- 1 **cup walnuts, finely chopped**

Mix together the flour, baking powder, baking soda and cinnamon using a fork. Beat eggs until a solid color; add sugar slowly. Keep beating until the mixture is light and fluffy. Then, add salad oil and vanilla; followed by dry ingredients, grated carrots and chopped nuts.

Bake in an ungreased 10-inch tube pan at 325° for 1 1/4 hours. Add favorite frosting.

Fruit Cake

2 1/2	cups candied cherries
2	cups candied pineapple
1/4	cup candied orange rind
1/4	cup candied lemon rind
1/2	cup candied citron
3	cups golden raisins
3/4	cup currants
1/2	cup brandy
1	cup shelled walnuts
3/4	cup blanched almonds
2	cups sifted all-purpose flour
1/2	teaspoon ground mace
1/2	teaspoon ground cinnamon
1/2	teaspoon baking soda
5	eggs
1	tablespoon milk
1	teaspoon almond extract
1/2	cup butter
1	cup sugar
1	cup brown sugar

Coarsely chop cherries, pineapple, orange rind, lemon rind and citron. Add raisins and currants; let fruit mixture soak overnight in brandy.

Coarsely chop walnuts and almonds; set aside.

The next day, line 10-inch tube pan with 2 layers of aluminum foil. Preheat oven to 275°.

Sift flour, measure 1 1/2 cups and sift with mace, cinnamon and baking soda onto wax paper. To prevent fruits from sticking, mix with remaining 1/2 cup flour.

Beat eggs slightly. Measure milk and almond extract into a cup. Cream butter well; add granulated sugar and cream till fluffy. Add brown sugar and cream well. Mix in eggs, milk mixture and flour thoroughly. Pour batter over fruits and nuts and blend. Fill tube pan.

Bake 3 hours and 15 minutes. Cool slightly and remove from pan. Remove foil while still warm.

Pound Cake

Does anybody know why this is called a "pound" cake? Does it weigh a pound? Do you pound the ingredients while making it? Or do you feel like pounding your fist on the kitchen table if it doesn't turn out good?

>   8   **eggs, separated**
>   6   **tablespoons sugar**
>   1   **pound butter**
> 2 3/4   **cups sugar**
> 3 1/2   **cups flour**
>   1/2   **cup light cream**
>   1   **tablespoon vanilla**

Beat egg whites until stiff with 6 tablespoons sugar. Place into the refrigerator.

Cream butter and sugar. Then, add egg yolks. Mix in flour and cream, alternating between each. Add vanilla. Fold in the beaten egg whites. Pour mixture into a large tube pan. Bake at 325° for about 1 1/2 hours.

Chocolate Cake

2	cups all-purpose flour
2	cups sugar
1	cup water
3/4	cup sour cream
1/4	cup butter
1	teaspoon vanilla extract
1/2	teaspoon baking powder
1 1/4	teaspoon baking soda
1	teaspoon salt
2	eggs
4	ounces unsweetened baking chocolate, melted

Measure all ingredients into a large bowl and beat for 1/2 minute at low speed, scraping the sides of the bowl frequently. Then, beat for 3 minutes at high speed. Pour into two 9-inch greased and floured cake pans. Bake in preheated oven at 350° for 20 to 25 minutes. Remove from oven and allow to cool on a rack.

Make filling and frosting as follows:

Frosting and Filling:

1/2	cup butter
4	ounces unsweetened baking chocolate
4	cups powdered sugar
1	cup sour cream
2	teaspoons vanilla extract

In top of a double boiler, melt butter and chocolate over barely simmering water. Remove from heat and cool. Add powdered sugar. Blend in sour cream and vanilla, beating until smooth.

Peach Cake

Topping:

- 1/2   cup sugar
- 4   tablespoons butter
- 1/2   teaspoon ground cinnamon
- 1/4   teaspoon nutmeg, grated
- 4   tablespoons butter

Using a fork, combine all of the ingredients for the topping in a bowl; set aside.

Cake:

- 4   tablespoons butter
- 1/4   cup sugar
- 1   egg
- 1   cup unbleached all-purpose flour
- 1 1/2   teaspoons baking powder
- 1/2   teaspoon salt
- 1/4   cup milk
- 3   ripe peaches, peeled and sliced

Preheat oven to 350°. Grease a 9-inch diameter pan.

Cream butter and sugar until light; beat in egg. Sift dry ingredients together. Beat half of dry ingredients into creamed mixture; beat in half of the milk. Repeat, beating well.

Pour batter into prepared pan. Arrange peach slices on top of batter. Bake for 25 minutes. Open oven and sprinkle topping over peaches. Close oven and bake for another 8 to 10 minutes, or until cake is firm and has pulled away from edges of the pan. Serve warm with heavy cream.

Whipped Cream Cake

1	cup pastry cream
1/2	cup egg whites
1	cup sugar
1 1/2	cups all-purpose flour
1 1/2	teaspoons baking powder
1/4	teaspoon salt
1	teaspoon vanilla

Whip the cream until stiff. Whip the egg whites until stiff. Combine whipped cream and eggs. Add the sugar slowly with a spoon. Sift together flour, baking powder and salt; add to mixture. Add the vanilla. Bake in 2 layers in well-buttered pans at 350° for 20 minutes.

Blueberry Cheese Pie

2	tablespoons cold water
2	tablespoons lemon juice
1	envelope plain gelatin
1/2	cup milk, scalded
2	egg yolks
1/3	cup sugar
2	cups creamed cottage cheese
1	9-inch graham cracker crust, chilled
1/2	cup currant jelly
1	pint blueberries

Place water, lemon juice and gelatin in blender. Cover and blend at low speed. Add hot milk. Push gelatin powder down with a spatula, if it sticks to the side of the container. When gelatin has fully dissolved, turn blender on high speed; add egg yolks, sugar and cottage cheese. Blend until creamy and smooth.

Pour into pie crust. Chill 2 hours or until firm. Melt currant jelly and stir until smooth; allow to cool. Stir berries into jelly. Spread over pie. Chill and serve.

Pecan Pie

4 tablespoons butter
3/4 cup brown sugar
3 eggs, unbeaten
3/4 cup light corn syrup
1 teaspoon lemon juice
1 cup pecans
1 9-inch pie shell, unbaked

Cream butter and brown sugar; add eggs and beat. Add corn syrup and lemon juice. Stir in pecans. Pour into unbaked pie shell.

Bake in preheated 450° oven 10 minutes; reduce heat to 325° and bake for 30 to 40 minutes more, until almost set in the middle. Shake pie to test if done.

Filbert Pie

3 eggs, slightly beaten
1 cup light corn syrup
1 cup light brown sugar
1 teaspoon vanilla
1/8 teaspoon salt
1 cup filberts, chopped
1 8-inch pie shell, unbaked

Combine all of the ingredients. Pour mixture into unbaked pie shell. Bake at 450° for 10 minutes; reduce heat to 325° and bake 30 minutes more, or until a knife inserted comes out clean.

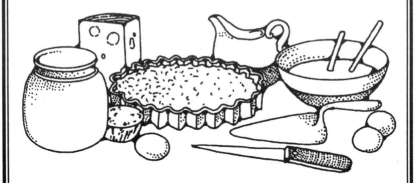

Pumpkin Pie

Simply incredible...

1	tablespoon gelatin
2/3	cup brown sugar
1 1/2	cups cooked pumpkin pie mix
1/2	teaspoon ginger
1/2	teaspoon cinnamon
1/2	teaspoon salt
3	egg yolks
1/2	cup sour cream
3	egg whites
1/2	cup sugar
1	9-inch pie shell, baked

Combine gelatin, brown sugar, pumpkin pie mix, ginger, cinnamon, salt and egg yolks in top of double boiler. Cook until it thickens. Pour into bowl and cool in refrigerator until lightly set, about 1 hour.

Mix in sour cream. Beat egg whites; add sugar and beat until thick. Fold egg whites and sugar mixture into pumpkin mixture. Spread into baked pie shell. Refrigerate 3 hours.

Strawberry Pie

4   **cups strawberries**
2/3 **cup sugar**
2   **teaspoons plain gelatin**
3   **tablespoons water**
1   **teaspoon lemon juice**
1   **9-inch pie shell, baked**

Purée 2 cups strawberries in blender. Strain through a sieve to remove seeds. Mix sugar and gelatin in saucepan. Stir in water and lemon juice. Stir over low heat until gelatin and sugar dissolve; combine with strawberry purée.

Chill purée mixture until consistency is slightly thicker than unbeaten egg white. Pour half of the mixture into pie shell. Arrange remaining 2 cups of strawberries in shell. Spread remaining purée mixture on top. Chill pie until set.

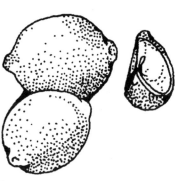

Lemon Pie

8   **eggs, separated**
2   **cups sugar**
    Juice of 3 lemons
2   **teaspoons lemon rind, grated**
1   **9-inch pie shell, baked**

Beat egg yolks in top of double boiler. Add 1 cup sugar, lemon juice and lemon rind. Mix together and cook over boiling water until thick, stirring constantly. Cool mixture.

Whip egg whites while adding 3/4 cup sugar. Mix 1/2 of egg whites into egg yolk mixture. Pour mixture into pie shell. Whip remaining 1/2 of egg whites with 1/4 cup sugar, and spread on top of pie. Bake at 375° for 5 to 8 minutes, until top is golden.

Apple Pie

        Tart apples, sliced
   1   **cup sugar**
   1   **teaspoon cinnamon**
  1/2 **teaspoon nutmeg**
   4   **tablespoons butter**

Line a pie pan with plain crust. Fill pan with thinly sliced apples. Mix together sugar, cinnamon and nutmeg; add to apples and stir together. Add butter in small pieces. Cover apple mixture with crust.

Bake at 375° for 3/4 to 1 hour until apples are tender, and crust is golden brown. Serve with ice cream.

Pear Pie

   4   **large pears**
   3   **tablespoons frozen orange juice**
  1/2 **cup sugar**
  1/3 **cup butter**
  3/4 **cup flour**
  1/2 **teaspoon cinnamon**
        Pinch of salt
   1   **9-inch pie shell, unbaked**

Peel pears and slice into pieces. Place slices into pie shell. Sprinkle frozen orange juice over slices. Mix together sugar, butter, flour, cinnamon and salt. Spread mixture over slices. Bake at 400° for 40 minutes.

Heavenly Pie

This "heavenly" pie won't get you into heaven, but after eating it you will feel like you are already there...

2 cups sugar
2 cups soda crackers, crushed
2 cups walnuts, chopped
1 tablespoon baking powder
7 egg whites
1 teaspoon vanilla

Mix together sugar, crackers, walnuts and baking powder. Beat egg whites until stiff. Fold in dry ingredients and vanilla into egg whites. Pour mixture into an 8-inch greased pie pan. Bake at 300° for 45 minutes, or until done.

Apple Crisp

Here's a delicious idea for all those apples on that tree out back...

6 cups cooking apples, pared and sliced
1/2 teaspoon salt
1 teaspoon cinnamon
1 tablespoon lemon juice
1 cup flour
1 cup light brown sugar
1 cup quick cooking rolled oats
2/3 cup butter

Pour 1/2 cup water into a large baking dish; spread in apples. Sprinkle apples with salt, cinnamon and lemon juice.

Mix together well the flour, brown sugar and oats. Mix in butter with a blender until the size of peas. Spread mixture over the apples, pressing down firmly.

Bake at 350° for 1 hour. Serve hot with your favorite ice cream and enjoy.

Berry Cobbler

3	cups blueberries or blackberries
3	tablespoons shortening
1 1/4	cups sugar
1	cup flour
1	teaspoon baking powder
1/4	teaspoon salt
1/2	cup milk
1	tablespoon cornstarch
1	cup boiling water

Spread berries in greased 8-inch square pan. Cream shortening and 3/4 cup sugar together well. Sift flour, baking powder and salt together; add alternately with milk to creamed mixture. Spread batter over berries. Combine remaining sugar and cornstarch for topping; sprinkle over batter. Pour boiling water over all. Bake at 350° for 1 hour. Serve with whipped cream or ice cream.

Meringue Tart

	Cream of tartar
3	egg whites
1	teaspoon vanilla
1	teaspoon vinegar
1	teaspoon water
1/2	teaspoon baking powder
1/8	teaspoon salt
1	cup sugar

Add a little cream of tartar to three egg whites; set aside. Combine in a cup the vanilla, vinegar and water. Using an electric mixer at high speed, combine egg mixture, vanilla mixture, and remaining ingredients, except sugar. When egg whites are very stiff, add sugar a tablespoon at a time.

Butter a pie plate. Shape the meringue like a pie. Bake at 275° for 1 hour or longer. Cool on rack. Fill with whipped cream, fruit or ice cream.

Apricot Soufflé

1	8-ounce package dried apricots
1	12-ounce can apricot nectar
5	egg whites, stiffly beaten
1/4	teaspoon salt

Place dried apricots and apricot nectar in a saucepan. Simmer until apricots are very soft. Purée and allow to cool completely. Butter a soufflé dish, and sprinkle the sides and bottom with powdered sugar.

Beat egg whites with salt until they hold a peak. Fold part of the beaten egg whites into the apricot purée to lighten. Then, fold mixture into the egg whites. Pour mixture into the soufflé dish.

Place soufflé dish in shallow pan of hot water. Bake at 350° for about 40 minutes.

Banana Soufflé

- **6 ripe bananas**
- **7 tablespoons confectioners sugar**
- **1 tablespoon lemon juice**
- **1 teaspoon vanilla**
- **4 egg whites, beaten stiffly**
- **1/4 teaspoon salt**

Peel bananas and mash until smooth. Mix in sugar, lemon juice and vanilla, stirring thoroughly; set aside. Butter a 1 1/2 quart soufflé dish, and sprinkle the sides and bottom with granulated sugar.

Beat egg whites with salt until they hold a peak. Carefully fold egg whites into banana mixture, and pour into soufflé dish. Sprinkle the top with granulated sugar.

Place soufflé dish in shallow pan of hot water. Bake at 350° for 30 minutes, or until golden and puffy. Serve topped with chocolate sauce.

Caramel Custard

    8   egg yolks
    2   whole eggs
  3/4   cup sugar
    4   cups cream, scalded
    1   cup milk
    2   teaspoons vanilla
    1   pound brown sugar

Beat egg yolks and whole eggs, adding sugar a little at a time. Add scalded cream, milk and vanilla. Pour mixture into 9x13-inch baking dish. Set in pan of hot water.

Bake at 350° for about 1 hour until set, when an inserted knife comes out clean.

Sprinkle brown sugar on top, and put under broiler for a few minutes to melt sugar. Serve with fruit.

Baked Chocolate Pudding

  1/4   cup butter
  3/4   cup sugar
1 1/2   cups sifted all-purpose flour
2 1/2   teaspoons baking powder
  1/2   teaspoon salt
  3/4   cup milk
  3/4   cup walnuts, chopped
  1/4   cup cocoa powder
    1   cup brown sugar
    1   cup boiling water

Cream butter and sugar. Sift together flour, baking powder and salt. Then, alternating with milk, add flour mixture to the creamed mixture. Fold in walnuts. Pour the batter into a greased 8-inch baking pan. Mix cocoa powder and brown sugar. Sprinkle over the batter. Pour 1 cup boiling water over everything.

Bake at 375° for 40 minutes. Serve with whipped cream.

Persimmon Pudding

Pudding:

- **1** cup sugar
- **1/3** cube butter
- **1** egg, beaten
- **1/2** teaspoon salt
- **1** cup persimmon pulp
- **1/2** cup milk
- **1** cup flour
- **2** teaspoons soda
- **1** teaspoon cinnamon
- **1/2** teaspoon cloves
- **1** teaspoon vanilla

Cream together sugar and butter in a bowl. Add beaten egg, salt, persimmon pulp and milk; mix well. Add flour, soda, cinnamon, cloves and vanilla; mix well. Put into a greased pudding mold. Steam for 2 to 2 1/2 hours.

Foamy Hard Sauce:

- **1 1/2** cups powdered sugar
- **1/3** cup melted butter
- **1** egg, beaten
- **1/2** teaspoon vanilla
- **1** cup whipped cream
- **2** tablespoons rum

Mix together sugar and melted butter. Add beaten egg and vanilla. Fold in whipped cream. Stir in rum. Chill in refrigerator.

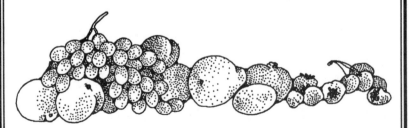

Popcorn Pudding

  2   **cups popped corn, pounded**
  3   **cups milk, scalded**
  3   **eggs**
1/2   **cup brown sugar**
  1   **teaspoon vanilla**
1 1/2 **tablespoons butter**
  1   **teaspoon mace**

Scald milk and pour over popped corn; let stand 1 hour. Blend eggs, brown sugar, vanilla, butter and mace. Stir mixture into the popped corn and milk mixture. Pour into a buttered pudding dish. Bake at 325° for 1 hour.

Strawberry Mousse

  2   **egg whites, room temperature**
1/4   **teaspoon cream of tartar**
      Pinch of salt
  2   **cups whipping cream**
1 1/4 **cups powdered sugar, sifted**
  2   **cups strawberries, puréed and chilled**
      Whipped cream (garnish)

Beat egg whites, cream of tartar and salt in small bowl until stiff and shiny; set aside. Whip 2 cups cream with sugar in bowl until stiff. Blend strawberry purée into the cream until mixture is very thick. Gently fold in egg whites, blending well.

Spoon mousse into individual serving dishes. Refrigerate at least 1 hour. Garnish with whipped cream just before serving.

Chocolate Mousse

The perfect ending for that "special" dinner...

> 1 **6-ounce package semi-sweet chocolate pieces**
> 2 **tablespoons orange juice**
> 2 **tablespoons coffee liqueur**
> 2 **egg yolks**
> 2 **eggs**
> 1 **teaspoon vanilla**
> 4 **tablespoons sugar**
> 1 **cup whipping cream**
> **Whipped cream (garnish)**

Melt chocolate, orange juice and coffee liqueur together in double boiler. With electric mixer beat eggs, vanilla and sugar about 1 1/2 minutes at medium speed. Add whipping cream; blend about 30 seconds. Add chocolate mixture and blend until smooth.

Spoon mousse into individual serving dishes and refrigerate. Garnish with whipped cream just before serving.

Swedish Cream

> 2 1/3 **cups heavy cream**
> 1 **cup sugar**
> 1 **envelope plain gelatin**
> 1 **pint sour cream**
> 1 **teaspoon vanilla**
> **Sweetened fruit or berries**

Combine cream, sugar and gelatin in saucepan. Heat gently and stir until gelatin is dissolved. Cool until slightly thickened. Fold in sour cream and vanilla. Chill until firm. Top with sweetened fruit or berries.

Vanilla Ice Cream

        2   cups milk
        2   tablespoons flour
        2   tablespoons water
      3/4   cup sugar
        2   egg yolks, beaten
        1   cup heavy cream
        1   teaspoon vanilla

Scald milk while stirring constantly. Mix flour and cold water together into a smooth paste. Slowly add to this paste the scalded milk, continuing to stir. When thickened, cook over hot water for 15 minutes. Add sugar and beaten egg yolks, cooking two minutes.

Strain mixture through a fine sieve. Allow it to cool to room temperature. Then, add heavy cream and vanilla. Place in freezer. Serve with your favorite topping, sauce or fruit.

Cherry Jubilee

Folks, keep your fire extinguisher handy for this one...

        1   cup preserved pitted Bing or other cherries
        1   teaspoon cornstarch
      1/4   cup brandy, slightly warmed
        2   tablespoons kirsch

Heat cherries to boiling in a pan. After cherries are boiling well, mix in cornstarch. Add slightly warmed brandy. Set brandy on fire. After flame has died down, add the kirsch. Sauce may be served hot over vanilla ice cream.

Chocolate Chip Cookies

Granny hid these under the bed and in other secret "hard-to-find" places, but sometimes even <u>she</u> couldn't find them later...

1 cup butter, softened
1 cup brown sugar
1/2 cup sugar
2 eggs
1 teaspoon vanilla
2 cups all-purpose flour
1 teaspoon baking soda
1 teaspoon salt
2 cups semi-sweet chocolate chips

Cream together butter and both sugars until light and fluffy. Add eggs and vanilla; mix well. Sift dry ingredients together and stir in; mix well. Add chocolate chips. Drop teaspoonfuls of dough onto a greased cookie sheet.

Bake cookies in a preheated 350° oven for 8 to 10 minutes, removing cookies from the oven when centers are slightly soft. Cool on baking sheet 5 minutes; then transfer cookies to rack to cool completely.

Chocolate Macaroons

        2   ounces unsweetened chocolate
        1   14-ounce can sweetened condensed milk
        1   cup nuts, chopped
        2   cups coconut, finely shredded
        1   tablespoon brewed coffee
        1   teaspoon almond extract
      1/8   teaspoon salt

In a heavy saucepan, combine the chocolate and milk. Cook over medium heat, stirring briskly until thick and shiny. Remove from heat. Add the remaining ingredients, stirring to blend well.

Drop the mixture by teaspoonfuls on a greased cookie sheet about 1-inch apart. Bake at 350° for 10 minutes, or until the bottoms are set. Be careful not to bake too long, macaroons should be soft and chewy. Remove to waxed paper to cool.

Lyngen Cookies

        1   cup white sugar
        1   cup brown sugar
        1   cup shortening (1/2 butter)
        1   cup salad oil
        1   egg
        1   teaspoon vanilla
    3 1/2   cups flour
        1   teaspoon salt
        1   teaspoon soda
        1   teaspoon cream of tartar
        1   cup rice crispies
        1   cup oatmeal

Cream both sugars, shortening, salad oil, egg and vanilla together. Add remaining ingredients to mixture in the order listed.

Form into walnut-sized balls. Place on a greased cookie sheet. Press down dough with fork. Bake at 350° for 10 minutes, or until lightly browned.

Gingerbread Cookies

During the Christmas holidays, granny couldn't bake these cookies fast enough to keep the cookie jar full. Come to think of it, they usually never <u>made</u> it into the cookie jar...

2 1/4	cups dark corn syrup
1	cup butter
1 1/2	cups brown sugar
1/2	cup shortening
8 3/4	cups sifted flour
1 1/2	teaspoons ginger
1 1/2	teaspoons cinnamon
3/4	teaspoon cloves
3/4	teaspoon nutmeg
1	teaspoon coriander
1/2	teaspoon pepper
1/2	teaspoon cardamom
4	egg yolks, beaten
1	teaspoon baking soda
2 1/2	teaspoons baking powder

Combine corn syrup, butter, brown sugar and shortening in a saucepan; bring mixture to a boil. Remove from heat. Then, add 3 3/4 cups of sifted flour, ginger, cinnamon, cloves, nutmeg, coriander, pepper and cardamom. Mix together well until the dough comes away from the sides of pan. Let dough cool to room temperature.

Then, add the beaten egg yolks, and 5 cups flour sifted with baking soda and baking powder. Use your hands to mix the dough. Once mixed, turn dough onto a lightly floured surface and knead until it becomes shiny.

Roll dough out onto a floured surface until it becomes very thin. Cut out dough with different shapes of cookie cutters. Place on a greased cookie sheet. Brush dough with a beaten egg to make cookies shiny.

Bake at 350° for 10 minutes or until lightly browned; be careful not to burn cookies.

Cream Cheese Cookies

    1   **cup butter**
    3   **ounces cream cheese**
    1   **teaspoon vanilla**
    1   **egg yolk**
    1   **cup sugar**
2 1/2   **cups flour**

Cream butter and cream cheese together. Add vanilla and egg yolk. Add sugar and mix together well. Blend in flour. Roll out dough on a floured board. Cut with cookie cutter, and place on a greased cookie sheet. Bake at 375° for 10 to 15 minutes. Ice cookies with colored icing if desired.

Almond Cookies

    2   **cups almonds, shelled**
    1   **cup sugar**
    2   **egg whites**

Boil shelled almonds until the skins loosen; drain. While almonds are still hot, remove the skins. Put almonds through a food processor with the finest blade; blend in sugar well. Beat egg whites until stiff; fold into almond mixture. Drop by teaspoonfuls onto a floured cookie sheet. Bake at 375° for 10 to 12 minutes.

Praline Cookies

    1   cup dark brown sugar, firmly packed
    3   tablespoons butter, melted
    5   tablespoons flour
    1   cup pecan halves
    1   egg, beaten
    1   teaspoon vanilla
        Pinch of salt

Combine butter and brown sugar. Mix in well the flour, pecans, egg, vanilla and salt. Grease a cookie sheet and coat with flour. Drop dough by teaspoonfuls onto sheet, 5 inches apart. Top each with a pecan half.

Bake at 350° for 8 to 10 minutes. To prevent sticking, remove cookies from sheet after 1 minute and cool on rack.

Pretzel Cookies

    2   cups pretzel sticks, broken into short pieces
    1   pound white chocolate
    1   cup Spanish peanuts

Melt white chocolate. Mix in broken pretzel pieces and peanuts. Drop by teaspoonfuls onto wax paper. Allow to cool.

Oatmeal Coconut Cookies

       2 **egg whites**
     1/2 **teaspoon cream of tartar**
     1/4 **teaspoon salt**
       1 **cup sugar**
       1 **cup shredded coconut, unsweetened**
       2 **tablespoons butter, melted**
       1 **cup rolled oats**
       1 **teaspoon vanilla**

Beat the egg whites with cream of tartar and salt until stiff, but not dry. Slowly beat in the sugar. Fold in coconut, butter, rolled oats and vanilla.

Drop by teaspoonfuls onto a greased cookie sheet. Bake at 350° for 15 minutes.

Honey Cookies

       1 **cup soft butter**
     1/4 **cup honey**
     1/2 **teaspoon vanilla**
       2 **cups all-purpose flour, sifted**
       1 **teaspoon cinnamon**
       1 **cup hazelnuts, finely chopped**
          Icing sugar

Cream butter, honey and vanilla together until well blended. Sift flour and cinnamon together into creamed mixture and blend well. Blend in the hazelnuts. Chill in refrigerator for several hours. Preheat oven to 325°.

Shape dough into walnut-sized balls and put onto an ungreased cookie sheet. Bake for 15 to 18 minutes, or until golden and set.

Cool cookies on racks for several minutes, then roll in icing sugar. Allow cookies to cool completely, and roll in icing sugar again before storing.

Caramel Cookies

        1   cup shortening
        1   cup sugar
       1/2   cup brown sugar
        3   eggs
        2   teaspoons vanilla
       1/2   teaspoon baking soda
        1   teaspoon salt
        5   cups all-purpose flour, sifted

Cream the shortening. Blend in the sugar and brown sugar gradually, while beating well. Add the eggs and vanilla to mixture. Sift together baking soda, salt and flour. Add sifted ingredients to mixture gradually.

Drop dough by teaspoonfuls onto an ungreased cookie sheet. Bake at 375° for 8 to 10 minutes.

Peanut Butter Cookies

       1/2   cup peanut butter
       1/2   cup shortening
       1/2   cup brown sugar, packed
       1/2   cup sugar
       1/2   teaspoon vanilla
        2   eggs, slightly beaten
        1   teaspoon baking powder
       1/2   teaspoon baking soda
       1/2   teaspoon salt
      1 1/2 cups all-purpose flour, sifted

Mix together peanut butter and shortening until blended well. Blend in sugar and brown sugar gradually. Add vanilla and eggs. Sift together baking powder, baking soda, salt and flour. Add sifted ingredients to mixture gradually; mix well together.

Form dough into walnut-sized balls. Place on an ungreased cookie sheet. Press dough with a fork to form ridges. Bake at 375° for 10 minutes or until cookies are golden brown.

Coffee Cookies

- 1 cup sugar
- 1 cup butter
- 2 eggs, beaten
- 1 cup molasses
- 1 cup hot coffee
- 1 tablespoon vinegar
- 4 cups all-purpose flour, sifted
- 1 teaspoon salt
- 2 teaspoons soda
- 1 teaspoon ginger

Cream together the sugar and butter until fluffy. Add the eggs, molasses, hot coffee and vinegar. Combine mixture with the flour, salt, soda and ginger; blend well.

Drop dough by teaspoonfuls onto a greased cookie sheet. Bake at 375° for 10 minutes.

Lace Cookies

1/3	cup flour
1/4	teaspoon baking powder
1/2	cup sugar
1/2	cup quick-cooking oat meal
2	tablespoons cream
1/3	cup butter, melted
2	tablespoons light corn syrup
1	teaspoon vanilla

Sift together flour, baking powder and sugar. Add oats, cream, butter, light corn syrup and vanilla. Mix well.

Drop 1/4 teaspoon of dough well apart on a greased cookie sheet. Bake at 375° for 6 to 7 minutes.

Orange Cookies

2	cups sugar
3	cups margarine
2	eggs
6	cups flour
2	teaspoons baking soda
2	teaspoons orange extract

Cream margarine and sugar. Add eggs and beat well. Add sifted flour and baking soda. Then, add orange extract.

Drop by teaspoon onto a greased cookie sheet. Bake at 325° until golden brown.

Apricot Squares

- 3 tablespoons butter
- 3 tablespoons cream
- 1/4 cup sugar
- 1 egg
  Pinch of salt
- 1 cup flour
- 2 teaspoons baking powder
- 1 teaspoon vanilla
  Apricots, halved

Crumb Topping:

- 1/2 cup flour
- 1/2 cup sugar
- 3 tablespoons butter
- 1 teaspoon vanilla

Cream together butter, cream, sugar, egg and salt. Add flour and baking powder, then vanilla. Press dough into a greased pan. Cover with halved apricots. Top with crumb topping. Bake in 375° oven for 30 to 35 minutes. Cut into squares and enjoy.

Cracker Squares

50	Ritz crackers
6	egg whites
1 1/2	cups sugar
2	teaspoons vanilla
1	cup nuts, chopped
1	teaspoon coconut
2	cups whipped cream
	Sweet chocolate, grated

Roll crackers until fine. Beat egg whites until stiff; add sugar gradually. Stir in vanilla and nuts. Pour mixture into a buttered 9x13-inch cake pan. Bake at 350° for 20 minutes. Allow to cool.

Fold coconut into whipped cream. Spread whipped cream on top. Put grated sweet chocolate on top. Chill in refrigerator. Cut into squares and serve.

Walnut Squares

2	eggs, beaten
2	cups brown sugar
2	cups walnuts, chopped
1	teaspoon vanilla
10	tablespoons flour
1/4	teaspoon salt
1/4	teaspoon soda

Mix all ingredients. Pat into a greased 9x9-inch pan. Bake in oven at 325° for 20 to 25 minutes, or until an inserted toothpick comes out clean. Cut into squares.

Brownies

The dough is so good, it may get eaten before it gets into the oven!

- 1   **cup butter**
- 4   **ounces unsweetened chocolate**
- 4   **eggs**
- 2   **cups sugar**
- 1   **teaspoon vanilla**
- 1/2 **cup all-purpose flour**
- 1/4 **teaspoon salt**
- 1/2 **cup walnuts, coarsely chopped**

Melt butter and chocolate in the top of a double boiler over boiling water. When melted, set aside the mixture and cool to room temperature.

Beat eggs and sugar until thick; add vanilla. Fold chocolate mixture into eggs and sugar; mix thoroughly. Sift flour; fold flour and salt into batter, mixing until blended. Fold in walnuts.

Pour into a well-greased 9x13-inch pan. Bake in preheated 350° oven for 25 minutes, or until center is just set. Do not overbake. Allow to cool for 30 minutes. Cut into squares.

Caramel Fudge

    2   cups sugar
    1   6-ounce can evaporated milk
    2   tablespoons light corn syrup
    1   10-ounce jar vanilla caramel sauce
    1   teaspoon vanilla
  1/4   teaspoon maple flavoring
  1/2   cup walnuts, chopped

Butter the sides of a heavy 2-quart saucepan. Combine in saucepan the sugar, milk, corn syrup and caramel sauce. Heat and stir over medium heat until sugar dissolves and mixture begins to boil. Then, cook to soft-ball stage at 235°, stirring occasionally. Remove from heat.

Stir in vanilla and maple flavoring; beat just until mixture begins to lose its shine. Stir in walnuts. Pour into a buttered 8x8x2-inch pan. Score fudge while still warm; then cut into squares when firm.

Peanut Butter Fudge

    2   cups sugar
  2/3   cup milk
  1/2   pint jar marshmallow creme
    1   cup chunky peanut butter
    1   6-ounce package semi-sweet chocolate
    1   teaspoon vanilla

Butter sides of a heavy 2-quart saucepan. Combine in saucepan the sugar and milk. Heat and stir over medium heat until sugar dissolves and mixture comes to boiling. Cook to soft-ball stage at 235°, stirring occasionally. Remove from heat.

Add remaining ingredients and stir until blended. Pour into a buttered 9x9x2-inch pan. Score fudge while still warm; then cut into squares when firm.

Peanut Cluster Bars

- 1 12-ounce package chocolate chips
- 1 12-ounce package butterscotch chips
- 1 cup peanut butter
- 12 ounces unsalted peanuts
- 1 10-ounce bag miniature marshmallows

Melt chocolate and butterscotch chips in top of double boiler; add peanut butter and stir to blend. Combine nuts and marshmallows in bowl; add chocolate mixture and toss to coat evenly. Press into buttered 9x13-inch pan. Chill. Cut into squares.

Lemon Bars

Crust:

- 2 cups flour
- 1/2 cup powder sugar
- 1 cup soft margarine

Mix flour, sugar and margarine; press into a 9x13-inch pan. Bake at 350° for 15 minutes.

Filling:

- 4 eggs
- 2 cups sugar
- 1/3 cup lemon juice
- 1/4 cup flour
- 1/2 teaspoon baking powder

Mix all ingredients. Pour over crust. Bake at 350° for 20 to 25 minutes. Sprinkle with powdered sugar.

Almond Chocolate Bars

Bet you can't eat just one...

1	cup butter
1/2	cup brown sugar
1/2	cup sugar
1	egg yolk
1	cup flour
1	teaspoon baking powder
6	1.5-ounce chocolate bars
1 1/2	cups almonds, finely chopped

Cream together butter and both sugars. Add egg yolk and blend. Combine flour and baking powder; add to above mixture. Spread evenly in a 9x13-inch pan. Bake at 325° for 25 minutes.

Remove from oven, and quickly arrange the chocolate bars on top. Spread evenly as the chocolate softens, then sprinkle with chopped nuts. Cut while warm. Refrigerate to set. Serve bars at room temperature.

Chocolate Meringue Bars

1	6-ounce package semi-sweet chocolate chips
2	egg whites
	Dash of salt
3/4	cup powdered sugar
1/2	teaspoon vanilla
1/2	teaspoon white vinegar
1/2	cup walnuts, chopped

Melt chocolate chips over low heat. Beat egg whites with salt until fluffy. Gradually add sugar, beating continuously until stiff and shiny. Beat in vanilla and vinegar. Gently fold in melted chocolate and nuts.

Drop with a teaspoon onto an ungreased cookie sheet. Bake at 350° for 10 minutes. Cool on rack.

Butterscotch Meringue Bars

1/4	cup butter
1	cup brown sugar
1	egg
1/2	teaspoon vanilla
3/4	cup sifted all-purpose flour
1/2	teaspoon salt
1/4	teaspoon nutmeg
1	egg white
1	tablespoon light corn syrup
1/2	cup sugar
1/2	cup walnuts, chopped

Combine butter and brown sugar. Cook and stir over low heat until mixture begins to bubble; allow to cool. Add egg and vanilla, beating well. Sift together flour, salt and nutmeg. Stir into sugar mixture. Spread dough in a greased 8x8x2-inch pan.

Beat egg white to soft peaks; gradually add corn syrup. Then, gradually add sugar, beating to stiff peaks. Fold in walnuts. Spread mixture over dough. Bake at 350° for 30 minutes. Cut into bars.

Lady Fingers

5	tablespoons powdered sugar
3	egg whites, stiffly beaten
2	egg yolks, well beaten
1/2	teaspoon vanilla
1/2	cup flour
1/4	teaspoon salt
	Powdered sugar

Add powdered sugar to beaten egg whites. Add beaten egg yolks and vanilla. Sift flour twice with salt. Fold in the flour to the mixture. Line a pan with ungreased paper.

Press batter onto pan through a pastry bag, forming 1x4-inch strips. Sprinkle with powdered sugar. Bake at 350° for 10 minutes.

Chocolate Rolls

6	egg whites
	Dash of salt
1/3	cup sugar
1/3	cup cocoa
	Whipped cream

Beat egg whites until stiff; add salt, sugar and cocoa. Cover a cookie sheet with greased paper. Spread mixture on cookie sheet about 8 inches wide. Bake at 300° for 15 to 20 minutes.

Remove from oven. Spread with whipped cream and roll like a jelly roll. Chill in refrigerator. Slice and serve.

Strawberry Puffs

Puffs:

- 1 **cup boiling water**
- 1/2 **cup butter**
- 1 **cup all-purpose flour**
- 1/4 **teaspoon salt**
- 4 **eggs**

Melt butter in boiling water. Add flour and salt, stirring vigorously. Cook and stir until mixture forms a stiff ball. Remove from heat and allow to cool slightly. Add eggs one at a time, beating well after each egg is added until smooth.

Drop by tablespoonfuls 4-inches apart on a greased cookie sheet. Bake at 450° for 15 minutes, then at 325° for 25 minutes. Allow to cool. Split puffs and remove webbing.

Filling:

- 1 **cup dairy sour cream**
- 1/4 **cup sugar**
- 2 **cups miniature marshmallows**
- 1 **quart strawberries**

Mix together sour cream, sugar and marshmallows. Cover and chill for several hours.

Wash and hull the strawberries. Crush 2 cups of the strawberries, and slice the remaining. Fold all of the strawberries into the chilled cream mixture. Fill each puff with 1/4 cup strawberry filling.

Danish Puffs

Puffs:

- 1 **cup margarine**
- 2 **cups flour, sifted**
- 2 **tablespoons cold water**
- 3 **eggs**
- 1 **cup boiling water**

Cut 1/2 cup margarine into 1 cup flour. Add 2 tablespoons cold water and stir well to blend. Split dough in halves. Form each half into a 3x12-inch shape on an ungreased cookie sheet.

Place 1 cup boiling water and remaining margarine in saucepan, and bring to boil. Remove from heat, and stir in remaining flour. Add eggs one at a time, beating well after each is added. Spread mixture over dough on cookie sheet.

Bake at 425° for about 50 minutes. Meanwhile, make the frosting.

Frosting:

- 2 **cups powdered sugar**
- 1 **tablespoon margarine**
- 4 **tablespoons cream**
- 1 **teaspoon vanilla**
- 1/8 **teaspoon salt**

Combine sugar, margarine, cream, vanilla and salt. Beat mixture until smooth. Frost cakes while hot. Cut into slices.

Cream Puffs

- 1 **cup water**
- 1/2 **cup butter**
- 1 **cup all-purpose flour**
- 1/4 **teaspoon salt**
- 4 **eggs**
  Whipped cream

Place the water and butter in a saucepan and heat until boiling. Add flour and salt to the mixture, while beating thoroughly. Stir and cook over low heat until mixture forms a stiff ball. Remove from heat and add the unbeaten eggs one at a time, beating thoroughly after each is added.

Drop by teaspoonfuls (for small puffs) or by tablespoonfuls (for larger puffs) on a greased cookie sheet.

If baking small puffs, bake at 450° for 15 minutes, then at 325° for 20 minutes. If baking large puffs, bake at 450° for 20 minutes, then at 325° for 20 minutes.

Split puffs and fill with whipped cream.

Mints

 1/3   **cup butter**
 1/3   **cup light corn syrup**
   1   **teaspoon peppermint flavoring**
 1/2   **teaspoon salt**
   1   **pound confectioners sugar, sifted**
       Red food coloring

Combine butter with corn syrup, peppermint flavoring and salt in a large bowl. Add sugar and mix together with a spoon. Knead mixture well with hands. Add food coloring. Roll out flat and cut into rounds using a cookie cutter.

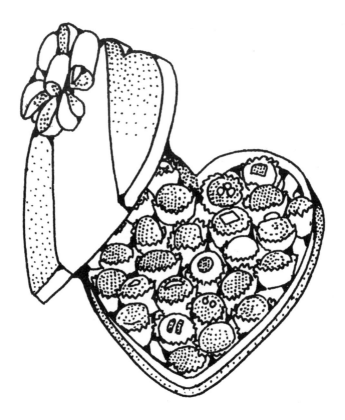

Chocolate Strawberries

Mmmmmmmm....yummy!

2 cups firm strawberries
1 12-ounce package semi-sweet chocolate pieces

Rinse strawberries well and dry on paper towels. Do not remove the stems.

Melt chocolate pieces over hot water in a double boiler. Stir until smooth; reduce heat. Dip strawberries in chocolate one at a time, leaving an uncoated rim around the stem. Shake off extra chocolate and place on wax paper. Refrigerate about 30 minutes to set. Serve strawberries in bonbon cups or on paper doilies.

Chocolate Cherries

These tasty treats will <u>really</u> make you pucker up!

     8   tablespoons butter, melted
     6   tablespoons corn syrup
     1   can milk
     1   teaspoon vanilla
     3   pounds powdered sugar
   100   maraschino cherries
     1   square paraffin
     1   large bag semi-sweet chocolate chips

Mix together well the butter, corn syrup, milk and vanilla. Add the powdered sugar and beat mixture until blended well. Knead with hands and form into balls, putting a cherry inside each ball. Place cherry balls in the freezer for one hour.

Melt the paraffin. Add the chocolate chips and melt in the top of a double boiler. Then, dip cherry balls into chocolate. Place on waxed paper and allow to cool.

Bonbons

     1   cup currant jelly
     1   envelope plain gelatin
   1/2   cup water
     1   cup semi-sweet chocolate chips

Grease a 8x8-inch pan. Melt the currant jelly over hot water in a double boiler using medium heat. Soften the gelatin in the water, and add to jelly; mix together well. Pour mixture into pan. Chill in refrigerator until very firm.

Cut jelly into small cubes the size of sugar cubes or larger if desired. Melt chocolate chips over hot water in the double boiler. Allow chocolate to cool until lukewarm. Dip cubes of jelly into the chocolate. Place bonbons on waxed paper and allow to cool.

Toffee

2   **cups sugar**
1 1/2   **cups corn syrup**
1 1/2   **cups light cream**
  Pinch of salt
4   **tablespoons butter**
1   **teaspoon vanilla extract**

Mix together sugar with corn syrup, cream and salt. Heat mixture and stir until the boiling point is reached. Continue cooking, stirring occasionally, until the mixture forms a ball when tried in cold water. Add butter and cook again until the mixture forms a hard ball when tried in cold water. Add vanilla before removing from heat.

Pour into a well-buttered pan and mark into rectangular shapes. The creases should be deep enough to allow candy to be separated easily. Wrap each piece in waxed paper.

Old-Fashioned Caramels

Homemade candies somehow seem to taste a whole lot better than ones bought from the store, especially when granny made them...

1   **cup cream**
2   **tablespoons flour**
1   **cup brown sugar**
1   **cup molasses**
1   **tablespoon butter**
1/2   **pound bitter chocolate**
1   **teaspoon vanilla extract**

Blend cream with the flour. Add the brown sugar, molasses, butter and chocolate. Heat mixture and boil until the candy hardens when tried in cold water. Then, add the vanilla and stir rapidly. Pour into a well buttered pan. When candy is nearly cool, mark into squares.

Caramel Apples

   1   **14-ounce can condensed milk**
   1   **cup sugar**
1/2   **cup light corn syrup**
1/8   **teaspoon salt**
   1   **teaspoon vanilla**
   6   **apples**
   6   **wooden sticks**

Grease a cookie sheet. In a heavy 2-quart saucepan, mix together milk, sugar, light corn syrup and salt. Over low heat, cook mixture and stir constantly until it boils and the sugar has dissolved. Keep cooking over low heat while constantly stirring, until mixture reaches the soft-ball stage (232°) on a candy thermometer. Remove mixture from heat. Add vanilla while stirring; allow to cool for 5 minutes.

Insert wooden sticks into apples. Dip apples into caramel and cover well. Place apples on the cookie sheet and allow to cool.

Salt Water Taffy

The kids will have loads of fun helping you make this candy...

- 2 **cups sugar**
- 1 **tablespoon cornstarch**
- 3/4 **cup water**
- 1 **cup light corn syrup**
- 2 **tablespoons butter**
- 1 **teaspoon salt**
   Flavoring and food coloring of your choice

Grease a cookie sheet with butter. Place sugar and cornstarch into a saucepan. Add water, corn syrup and butter. Heat and stir the mixture until it reaches boiling point. Boil without stirring, until mixture reaches the firm-ball stage (266°) on a candy thermometer. Add the salt. Pour mixture onto the cookie sheet. Allow taffy to cool until it can be handled.

Pull taffy until it becomes light colored. Split up taffy into different portions. Each portion can be flavored and colored by pulling the taffy until additives blend in. Flavorings may be lemon, strawberry, orange, peppermint or other flavorings of your choice. Color the taffy to match the flavor. Pull off taffy pieces and wrap in waxed paper. Place taffy in a closed container.

Crunchy Peanuts

- 1 **cup sugar**
- 1/2 **cup water**
- 2 **cups raw peanuts**

Pour water into a frying pan. Allow sugar to dissolve in water using medium heat. Add raw peanuts; continue to cook on medium-high heat while constantly stirring. Peanuts are done when they have a glazed and pinkish look.

Spread out peanuts on foil and allow to cool. Separate peanuts while they are still warm, to prevent sticking together. After peanuts have cooled, store in a closed container.

Peanut Brittle

       2   cups sugar
     1/2   cup light corn syrup
     1/2   cup water
     1/8   teaspoon salt
     1/8   teaspoon soda
       3   tablespoons butter
       2   cups peanuts
       1   cup coconut, shredded
     1/2   teaspoon vanilla

Place the sugar, corn syrup and water into a saucepan. Cook and stir until sugar has dissolved. Keep cooking until sugar begins turning light brown and reaches 300°. Remove mixture from heat.

Add the salt, soda and butter, stirring only slightly to mix well. Pour mixture over warmed nuts on a greased pan. Pour into thin sheets and smooth. After about 1/2 minute, pull brittle until it is very thin. Break into pieces.

Sugared Popped Corn

Pop some and bring it along to the movies...

       2   quarts popped corn
       2   tablespoons butter
       2   cups brown sugar
     1/2   cup water

Pop corn. Melt butter in a saucepan; add brown sugar and water. Bring to boiling point and allow to boil for 15 minutes. Pour over popped corn and mix well, coating every kernel. When dry, put away in a dry place.

Index